I have known Charlotte for over 20 years. During this time I have witnessed her Christian walk through years of trials and difficult struggles as a mother. Nevertheless, she never stopped holding on to God's hand and trusting in Him no matter what the cost. She was unwavering in her faith in God, as she continued to reflect His glory…and I witnessed it! There is no doubt that God was with her through it all, just like He has promised all of us. She truly demonstrated Hebrews 12:1-2 "Therefore since we are surrounded by such a great cloud of witnesses, let us throw off everything that hinders and the sin that so easily entangles. And let us run with perseverance the race marked out for us, fixing our eyes on Jesus…"

Charlotte ran that race and she is still shinning the LIGHT OF CHRIST with His power and glory leading the way.

She is such an example of how to walk with God through the tough times and as well as the blessed times. She's my soul sister.

I love you forever Charlotte!!

Debbie Lowmiller

I met Charlotte in 1997. We raised our children together on our little cul-de-sac. Charlotte was a dedicated, compassionate, and energetic mother. Simple hellos would turn into long meaningful conversations as you were always drawn to her cozy front porch. Sitting in her big rocking chairs or her wicker swing filled with her handmade cushions, her passion for the Lord and praying for her children was always evident in our conversations. Her love of Christ radiated in her expressive smiles and words as she poured her heart to you about her unwavering faith. She is an inspiration for parents to never give up and pray your children through the tough moments in their lives. Thank you, Charlotte for your testimony on living a victorious life in Christ and always making your home such an inviting place to come for prayer, encouragement, and friendship.

Nancy Estep

Joy! The seemingly unattainable euphoric state we all constantly pursue. Why is it so hard to find and why is it so hard to keep? Stress, tragedy, loneliness…we all battle something that if we let it could take over our lives. I've witnessed first-hand the pain Charlotte has endured for years. She yearned for her children to live full and joyous lives. The battle is so real. But through all her heart ache she soared, and soared so extremely high! God's love for her, and her love for the Lord brought her true peace and amazing joy at a time when most of us, including myself, would've faltered. This woman and this book should give you hope…hope for a future full of JOY!

I love you Charlotte!!

Keri Bailey

Charlotte, and I have been close personal friends for more than 37 years. I guess you could say, we are more like sisters from the bond we share. You see, Charlotte shared the gospel with me soon after we met in the early 1980's. I accepted Jesus Christ as my Lord and savior at that time and my life was permanently transfigured into a newness of life that I never knew existed.

Charlotte's oldest son was only two years old when we met, and since that time I have had many opportunities to witness firsthand her reactions and mannerisms in many different scenarios. Her loving example of being a born again Christian, and a wonderful devoted Mom, wife, and loyal friend has made a lifelong impact on me. She's a woman of integrity and true godly character.

Her smile and laughter are contagious. She's uninhibited, enthusiastic, and full of joy! I know the true joy Charlotte radiates comes from knowing Jesus as her personal Lord and Savior. She's the most genuine, true, "walk the walk and talk the talk" Christian, prayer warrior I have ever met. We've been there for each other through childbirth, weddings, happy times, and sad unexpected tragic life altering events. Through the years, Charlotte has proven to be a great example of a true, non-judgmental, humble, anointed Christian witness for the Lord. She's blessed with an innate ability to lead, listen, mentor, teach and encourage. I'm extremely grateful that the Lord put Charlotte in my life! What a blessing it has been to witness the power of Jesus transforming our lives and the lives of our families.

Grateful Believer of Jesus Christ,

Lisa Abney

LIVE IN THE VICTORY

God's Victorious Battle Plans for

Parents with Prodigals

Charlotte Jewell

ISBN: 978-1-945976-40-7

Published by EA Books Publishing, a division of Living Parables of Central Florida, Inc. a 501c3

EABooksPublishing.com

DEDICATION

This work is my book of remembrance and praise, dedicated to God the Father, Jesus Christ His divine Son, and the Holy Spirit, who empowers me every day of my life!

Also, my two warrior sons who have now found their own places of victory in the Lord Jesus Christ! They too have overcome by the word of their testimony and the blood of the Lamb. Through this unbelievably heart-wrenching journey, both of them have become the strong and "mighty warriors" I always prayed they would be! Oftentimes throughout my weary valley journey, the Lord would encouraged me with these words, "Your sons are in warrior training!" I soon realized that God was using our suffering to perfect our faith and to prepare all of us for His perfect will.

May Your will be done Lord Jesus in all our lives. Whatever brings You glory, whatever brings You praise and makes Your face radiate with joy...so be it! Amen!.

CONTENTS

Introduction

As I worked on the final edits of this book, the Lord gave me an amazing revelation of what happened the day I took an active role in the war that was destroying my family. It hit me like a shock wave as a friend of mine was sharing a dream she had. I knew it was God's word to the readers of this book. "In the dream," she said, "I was standing at a door, and there was a man standing there too, dressed in white."

She said she knew he was the one that was to open the door for her. Then he said to her, "Are you here to participate or just be a witness?" Three times he asked her that question. She wanted to say, "I am here to participate! But I don't know *how* to participate!"

Is this you right now? Do you want to participate in the fight against the enemy but don't know how? Do you know in your heart that God has the answers and He alone holds the only key to open the door to your victory, but you don't know what to do or how to actively participate in the battle? I believe God was asking my friend Lori the same question He is asking you: *Are you here to participate or just be a witness?*

If you are reading this book, you, like Lori, not only want to participate, you want to learn how to participate. You want to actively fight the way God wants you to fight. I believe with all my heart that you have come to the right place, and if you will follow God's strategic battle plans, you won't leave disappointed.

Unfortunately, many Christians, even strong Christians, become unwilling witnesses to the tragedy and trail of destruction the evil one brings into their lives because they never learn how to participate in the fight. First, we must realize that the war we're in is a spiritual war. Secondly, and most importantly, we need to learn how to do things God's way. If we believe He is the only one who can open that door, then we need to seek Him first to find out how to fight. If we don't seek Him for answers, not only will we not know what to do, but we will only be witnesses to the suffering and destruction the enemy leaves behind. Not only that, we'll find ourselves living from a place of defeat instead of victory, as we hopelessly watch the enemy destroy those we love.

This book contains God's victorious battle plans, the very plans He gave me to call back His destiny and purpose for my prodigal sons. For many of you, depending on where you are in your walk with the Lord, you may find yourselves standing at new doors of inspiration as you actively start implementing these plans.

As you read this book and witness the extraordinary victories and hope my family found in God's strategic battle plans, I pray you will be inspired to follow His victorious plans too. I believe that as you apply them to your own situation by actively participating with God, His strength will rise up in you, as it did in me, and cause you to persevere against the powers of hell every day. I have no doubt that you and your family will have the same incredible victories over the evil one as we did. Why am I so certain? Because my family's personal victories are living proof of what following God's instructions can do!

Now it's time to do your part and get in the fight!

1

Live in the Victory

The angel of the LORD encamps around those who fear him, and he delivers them (Psalm 34:7).

It happened when my faith was the strongest. When serving the kingdom was my business and leading souls to salvation my passion.

The threat could have only come from one place. And it wasn't good.

I'm gonna wipe that smile right off your face.

I heard it while driving home from church one night, where my ministry for teens was growing almost as fast as we could keep up with it. But I was ready for whatever the Devil had. Bring it on, I thought. I can take it.

But the Devil's plan was more cunning than I suspected. He knew my faith was strong, so he would attack where it hurt the most. Where I'd always hoped and prayed he wouldn't. But, yes, why *wouldn't* he go there . . . it made perfect sense.

Just a few months later, I watched my oldest son—my believing, Spirit-filled son—walk willingly into the world.

Behind enemy lines.

It was a battle my husband and I had not truly prepared for. We never really thought this would happen to us, not after the way we raised him.

We counter-attacked immediately by actively getting in the fight. The battles were daunting and dreadful as the war seemed to wage on forever. Satan and his forces of evil were relentless in their attempt to destroy our son's life. But we never fought alone. God took hold of our hands and walked with us, right onto the battlefield. Every day He gave us the battle instructions we needed and kept us covered with His shield of victory all through the fight. These battle instructions are what I want to share with you in this book, because I believe they were the essential keys to our victory.

As you read this book, please keep in mind that, while my husband was actively involved in the fight for our sons' victories over the enemy, this book was written from a mother's perspective. Most of what you are about to read was written during our fight for victory over the evil one. With that being said, let me continue with the story of how we overcame the enemy of our souls.

In the beginning, when the enemy first started his vicious attacks on my family, like most parents, we didn't know what to do! But I was willing and ready to do whatever God instructed me to do. So I watched and listened in careful desperation for any clues the Lord would send my way. I wanted to hear His voice and closely follow His instructions. Then, one day, I heard Him speak to me as clearly as if He'd spoken audibly.

It was mid-2003, and my son was in jail facing a gut-wrenching prison sentence. I had just finished praying, as I sat quietly before the Lord listening for His voice, suddenly, I heard Him speak, giving me my first and most powerful battle instruction. The Lord said, *Live in the victory. Don't wait until you have the victory to rejoice. But rejoice* now, *knowing that the victory is yours.* God was letting me know right from the start that He had already given me the victory, and my orders were to stand in faith, believing it was mine.

It's important that we understand that God already sees our lives from the beginning to the end. He doesn't live in time; He's our eternal God who created time. Therefore, He has already seen our life's ending as well as the beginning. He says, *I make known the end from the beginning, from ancient times, what is still to come* (Isaiah 46:10).

My friend, we must see this fight from the victory! Looking back now, without a doubt in my mind, I know He covered me with His shield of victory that day. *You have given me your shield of victory* (Psalm 18:35). From then on, that shield would be my covering, and I knew if I picked it up and took it into battle with me every day, it would be the protection I'd so desperately need. I began each day by taking up my shield of victory by faith. Then I'd walk out hand in hand with my Lord onto the battlefield to face the giants of that day.

In addition to all of these, hold up the shield of faith to stop the fiery arrows of the devil (Ephesians 6:16 NLT).

Each day, as I took up my shield and went into battle, I couldn't help but notice I felt as if I was in a place of complete safety. As though I was in a cocoon of sorts, surrounded with His protective covering all around me.

But you, LORD, are a shield around me, my glory, the One who lifts my head high (Psalm 3:3).

Believe me, there were some days when I just wanted to keep my head hung down in despair and defeat. I wanted to run away and hide somewhere far away from the watching world around me. But He kept me going and standing tall as He continued to surround me with His unfailing shield of victory and His perfect love. A love that casts out all fear.

There is no fear in love. But perfect love drives out fear (1 John 4:18).

***

The truth is, our kids are often the enemy's target because what better way is there to crush a parent's heart?

My children were raised in a godly, Christian home, where they were dearly and unconditionally loved and taught the ways of the Lord—not just in our words, but in our action as well. But now they were out of our protective care and making their own choices. It was up to them to decide which path they would follow. At this time in our lives, we had to learn to stand on the Word of God and His promises like never before, with unshakable faith.

Our hope was in God's living Word, and He had made us a very special promise:

Start children off on the way they should go, and even when they are old they will not turn from it (Proverbs 22:6).

Throughout my journey, the Word of the Lord and the promises I found in it sustained me because I knew this one thing to be true after all my years of serving the true and living God: *For no matter how many promises God has made, they are "Yes" in Christ. And so through him the "Amen" is spoken by us to the glory of God* (2 Corinthians 1:20). We say amen in agreement to the Word of God, who is our faithful anchor. When we come into agreement with Him, we are believing that He will perform His word and promises.

He is a promise keeper!

***

No matter what you're up against, no matter what you're going through, the only way out of the battle is to fight your way *through* it. If you're in the deep water, in over your head, you need deep-water faith to rise up. Let's face it: there's no room for shallow-water faith when you're in the deep end. It's time to learn how to swim and learn quickly.

When I found myself out in the deep, the Lord was quick to teach me what deep-water faith looked like. I must admit, I felt like I'd been thrown out in the middle of an ocean, but I wasn't alone. My lifeline was right there with me. Jesus let me know Satan's vicious attack on my family would ultimately prove futile. I'm so thankful He made this known to me right from the very beginning. He also gave me my life scripture verse at that same time. This verse would prove to be my prevailing guide and spiritual life preserver throughout the journey.

But seek first his kingdom and his righteousness, and all these things will be given unto you as well (Matthew 6:33).

This verse was not only my spiritual life preserver, it was the central place from which all of my battle strategies and plans would come. On the very day tragedy struck my home, I was given this scripture verse . . . or, you might say, this *order*. When I read it, I knew one thing for certain: I was to seek Him first before heading out into the battlefield (the world). This command was to be carried out throughout the war, no matter how long or weary the battle got. This was God's prevailing and sustained strategy for me if I wanted to not only survive this war but thrive throughout every battle and bring glory to Him. By seeking Him first, I was able to put everything in prioritized order and perspective; in essence, God was letting me know I just needed to keep Him at the forefront of my mind from the beginning of the war until the very end!

It was really a very simple concept when I thought about it. Kind of like the command He gave Adam and Eve . . . *only one tree to keep away from.* Only, in my case, it was only one *command* to keep at the forefront of my mind. The entire battle plan would hinge on this verse. Needless to say, as you read this book, you will discover how it became my prevailing theme throughout the entire war.

Oh yes, God was letting me know, from the very start, I was to seek Him first in every decision I made and live my life according to His righteous standards. Then all these things I was asking and praying for would be given to me! Basically, God was saying, "Go ahead and get excited every day as you go out into battle, because you are assured of a great victory if you will keep me at the forefront of all you do!" One thing I knew for sure, I was never to leave my post without Him first giving me His orders and then commanding me to move out!

Before long, I soon realized that this was my prevailing place of peace too. But if I allowed fear and doubt to enter into my post, I would lose my peace. In other words, God was telling me to make up my mind NOW if I was going to do it His way. For some reason, we always think we have to figure everything out. Please don't go there; He has it all figured out . . . trust me. I used to drive myself crazy in the beginning trying to figure it all out. That's like trying to write the next scene in a movie while you're still watching it, but somehow it never plays out the way you think it will. Especially the ending. So why drive yourself crazy trying to write the next scene in God's story? The Word of God says, *looking unto Jesus, the author and finisher of our faith* (Hebrews 12:2 NKJV). Let Him write the story of your life, while you follow His lead.

I must admit though, in the beginning of the war and several times throughout the many battles, I found it almost impossible to wait on the Lord for instruction. Now I know why He gave me that strict command early on: He was teaching me how to follow Him in strict obedience from the beginning until the very end! Let's face it: if it was going to be easy, then we could do it on our own power, not His. No, God gives us orders that seem earthly impossible so He can show us His mighty power as He divinely works through us.

God was also letting me know that if I didn't put Him first and follow His leading, it would take much longer to win each battle, let alone the entire war. Also, if I kept getting in the way by doing things my own way and leaning to my own understanding, the war would be much more difficult to win.

Trust in the LORD with all your heart and lean not to your own understanding; in all your ways submit to him, and he will make your paths straight (Proverbs 3:5-6).

Perhaps the Lord is saying the same thing to you today. Trust me when I say, doing things His way isn't always easy, nor does it make any sense often times. For example, rejoicing in the victory when all hell is breaking loose all around you in your life! But His Word says, *Rejoice in the Lord always* (Philippians 4:4). "With God all things are possible." God will give you the spiritual strength and strategies needed to face down your fiercest enemies and make what seemed literally impossible—possible! This tenacious strength is supernatural and completely impossible without God being first place in your life. Oh, but when you learn to submit to Him in this way, something absolutely amazing happens. An indescribable peaceful joy that surpasses all understanding sweeps over you like a holy covering:

And the peace of God, which surpasses all understanding, will guard your hearts and minds in Christ Jesus (Philippians 4:7 ESV).

My friend, when this happens to you, know that this is God's supernatural sign that you are winning even if you can't see victory anywhere in sight! This is a peace that goes beyond your understanding . . . God's prevailing peace! Yes, a peace that lets you know you are winning even if you can't see it yet with your natural eyes. Sometimes, when I knew I should be upset about something because in the natural realm it was completely overwhelming, for some crazy reason beyond my understanding I would have a wonderful peace about the situation. Then, suddenly, I would realize why I had this amazing peace and get very excited. Why? Because I soon began to understand that this was God's way of letting me know He was in the fight and we were winning! Actually, He was guarding my heart (mind, will, and emotions) during those times as I kept my mind focused on Him and not on my own understanding.

You will keep perfectly peaceful the one whose mind remains focused on you (Isaiah 26:3 ISV).

It was amazing how His supernatural peace seemed to flow through my soul like a gently flowing river, bringing with it a sweet calmness.

For this is what the LORD says: "I will extend peace to her like a river . . ." (Isaiah 66:12).

As you will hear me say over and over again throughout this book, we have an *active* part to play in this war, so actively keep your focus on Him.

Yes, He had already confirmed that absolute victory was coming our way. Now it was my job to believe it and keep my mind set on the victory. I understood the importance of my orders, and I knew how vital it would be for me to stay in a close relationship with my Lord at all times, especially if I wanted to keep learning how to swim in the deep waters I talked about earlier. Oh yes, God was telling me, *Set you mind. Stay in your set place with Me and don't go outside of it!*

Set your minds on things above, not on earthly things (Colossians 3:2).

On the day each of us was saved, we were immediately seated with Christ in heavenly places, via the Holy Spirit, and so we must remain heavenly minded. We are now operating from God's command post and using His kingdom principles and divine weapons of warfare to defeat our foes.

And God raised us up with Christ and seated us with him in the heavenly realms in Christ Jesus (Ephesians 2:6).

When my first order was given, I was right there by God's side, as He showed me it was time to armor up and march into battle. You see, I already had my earthly command center set up, a War Room, where I would pray and intercede to the throne of God on my son's behalf. This command center was the central place where the Lord would give me His strategic battle instructions. Then I would implement those instructions and activate the plan by faith.

Remember this: being active in the battle is a key and essential element if you're set on victory.

In the introduction, I shared with you my friend's dream and the question she was asked: "Are you here to participate, or just be a witness?" I knew that actively participating with God in the battle for my son's deliverance was my part to play in this war. And that, my friend, is how God taught me from the very beginning to live in the victory, even before I saw it, even before His promise of victory was fulfilled. Now He's instructing you to do the same thing. This is your first active-duty battle instruction, soldier: Seek God first for your instructions, and when the orders are given, MOVE OUT!

2

The Vision

Write the vision and make it plain . . . For the vision is yet for an appointed time; but at the end it will speak, and it will not lie. Though it tarries, wait for it; Because it will surely come (Habakkuk 2:2-3 NKJV).

In early January of 2003, only a few months before our war began, my husband installed a new car stereo and speakers he'd given me for Christmas. He anxiously called me out to the garage to listen to the new system. We got into my little convertible with the top down. Then he put in the new CD he'd given me by Michael W. Smith and selected the last song on the CD, which was all instrumental. As soon as the music played, I remember thinking, *this sounds heavenly*. As it continued to play, I became overwhelmed as the music seemed to wash over my soul in such a profound and unusual way.

By the time the music stopped, I knew in my spirit that all of heaven surrounded us. I didn't have to see it with my natural eyes—I could *feel* the Lord's presence overwhelming my spirit.

I turned to my husband, who sat in the driver's seat next to me and noticed tears were running down his face. I asked, "Honey, what just happened?" With his left arm still lifted toward heaven, he replied in a breathless tone, "Oh, Charlotte, I just felt the presence of the Lord so powerfully."

Although I had experienced the Lord's presence many times over my twenty-plus years of knowing Him, there was no doubt this was a special encounter. I knew the Lord was still actively moving in our midst.

So I asked my husband to play the song over. While he pressed the necessary buttons, I nestled down in my seat and settled my mind as I began worshiping, with my hands lifted toward heaven. Immediately, as the music played, once again it enchanted my soul. I was captivated by the awe and wonder of those heavenly sounds as they drew me deeper into worship.

It was indescribable and unlike anything I had ever heard.

What happened next is, admittedly, hard to believe. And, to be honest, if someone had shared this story with me early in my Christian life, I probably would have shut them down immediately. You may feel the same way. But I hope not, because the message that God brought that night is so important and definitely worth sharing. Not only that, it outlines the journey that, unbeknownst to us at the time, we would soon take with our prodigal child. And I believe it holds the same message for you too.

What happened was this: I was caught up in a vision.

Up until then, I'd never had a vision while completely awake. And I never have since. Normally, the Lord would show me things to come in night visions and dreams, much like Job talked about:

For God does speak—now one way, now another—though no one perceives it. In a dream, in a vision of the night, when deep sleep falls on people as they slumber in their beds, he may speak in their ears and terrify them with warnings . . . (Job 33:14-16).

Needless to say, this was something altogether different for me.

Then the Spirit lifted me up and brought me into the inner court, and the glory of the LORD filled the temple (Ezekiel 43:5).

Suddenly, I was completely immersed in a depth of worship that was beyond all definition or comprehension. Something supernatural was taking place. In an instant, I was in the spirit and taken up to what seemed like a mountaintop, where I found myself hand in hand with someone, caught up in a dance. I was leaning backward with my eyes closed as we gently swayed back and forth. Although I was aware that my body was still in the car, my spirit—the real Charlotte—was dancing with someone. As long as I live, I'll never forget how I felt in that glorious, celestial moment. I felt as though my spirit was immersed in the fullness of His joy and it was washing over me like a waterfall. I was wrapped in the inexpressible wonder of His presence.

As the dance continued, I felt completely one with this person. At first, because I came into the vision with my eyes closed and leaning backward, I didn't see whose hands I was holding. Then I wondered, *who am I dancing with?* As I opened my eyes and raised my head, I found myself gazing into the eyes of Jesus Christ! In that astonishing moment, He never said a word, nor was there a need for words—His love-filled, adoring eyes said it all! All I could see was unconditional *adoring love*! No one has ever looked at me like that! It made me feel like I was the most cherished person in all the world to Him. But I knew in my heart, it wasn't just a love for me—oh no. In that glorious moment, Jesus had revealed to me the depth of His love for all of humanity.

When the Word of God says, *God is Love* (1 John 4:8), believe me when I say, HE IS LOVE! His eyes and His presence personify love!

The LORD appeared to us in the past, saying: I have loved you with an everlasting love (Jeremiah 31:3).

It was as though in one brief, celestial moment of time, my eyes were opened to the eternal light of God's pure, unconditional love for His children.

After gazing into His eyes and being in His presence for only a few seconds, I found myself suddenly in what looked like a valley with lush green grass. I was dressed in white, and Jesus was holding on to my right hand, as He led me in a slow running motion through the valley. I looked in front of me to see where we were going, but I couldn't see anything in the distance except more green grass. Then I noticed someone was running along with us on the other side of Jesus, and Jesus was holding their hand too.

I leaned forward to see who it was. To my amazement, it was my husband, Steve. Jesus was holding both our hands, and He was leading us to some unknown place. Because I couldn't see what was in front of us, I had no idea of where we were going, but we were definitely being led someplace—somewhere completely unknown—by the hand of our Savior.

Then, just as quickly as I was taken up, the vision ended, and I was back in my body, sitting in the car with my husband. The awe and wonder of the experience still pulsated through my soul and spirit as I turned to my husband and muttered, "I just had a vision."

He listened intently as I told him about the vision and what had just happened to me, then we sat together, silently in awe, wondering what our encounter must have meant. One thing was for certain, though: we had both encountered our loving Savior and God that night in an inexpressible way. We both knew we would never be the same again.

After reading this, I know many of you may be thinking this sounds hard to believe. But, honestly, nothing I share with you in this book comes from anywhere but the Holy Word of God and what He has shown me. Again, the Word of God says, The LORD appeared to us in the past, saying: *"I have loved you with an everlasting love"* (Jeremiah 31:3).

Yes, the Lord has appeared to many others in the past, and even today. Throughout the Bible, in both the Old and New Testaments, people had similar experiences. In 2 Corinthians 12, the apostle Paul wrote: *I know a man in Christ who fourteen years ago was caught up to the third heaven. Whether it was in the body or out of the body I do not know—God knows. And I know that this man . . . was caught up to paradise and heard inexpressible things* (verses 2-4). From my own personal experience, I can understand why Paul said they were inexpressible: there just aren't words to describe what we saw or felt when we were in this heavenly place with the Lord.

If you find yourself standing at a new door in your spiritual walk with Jesus right now, please don't turn and walk away. He is the only one who can open that door and give you the understanding of this mystery. Why? Because, He is the door.

Most assuredly, I say to you, I am the door (John 10:7 NKJV).

As for me, after this experience, I couldn't wait to read and learn more about the visions documented in the Bible. Like I said before, as I began my study, I noticed there were numerous scriptures throughout the Old and New Testament describing others who were taken up in the spirit and shown the glory of God and things to come, much like I was. As I studied their experiences, I discovered that almost a third of the entire Bible was written due to spiritual encounters of one kind or another, including dreams and visions.

In the last days, God Says, I will pour out my Spirit on all people. Your sons and daughters will prophesy, your young men will see visions, your old men will dream dreams. (Acts 2:17)

This New Testament scripture is a fulfilment of what the prophet Joel prophesied in the Old Testament would happen in the last days (Joel 2:28). This tells me that God is still speaking to His people, even today, through visions and dreams, warning us of things yet to come. Although there is debate about when the last days began or will begin, according to what we are seeing now in the world, and what is written in the Word of God, I believe we are watching and living what was prophesied through the prophets of long ago. I truly believe we are living in the last of the last days!

Also, there's one significant thing I noticed while studying and reading about these godly encounters, when God sent a messenger or came Himself to someone—in whatever way, whether in a night vision (or dream as we call it) or a fully awake vision, He always had a good reason for the visit! And I know now that He had a very good reason for visiting us that evening too.

Before I go into more detail about why He came, I want to briefly clarify the difference between night visions or dreams, and fully awake visions. Actually, they are very much alike. The main difference is, night visions, which come in a dream-like state, take place when you're asleep, while visions take place when you're fully awake. Often times, visions need no interpretation, and eventually they play themselves out in our lives, giving us complete understanding. On the other hand, there are vivid dreams that have symbols, colors, and sometimes seem to us like a strange riddle. However, those dreams seem to stick with us, and in our spirit person we know they are from God. But they need interpretation. That's another reason God gave us the Holy Spirit and the Bible. He uses both to help us correctly understand the meaning of our dreams and visions. He also gave the ability to interpret dreams to certain people in the Bible, such as Daniel. Either way, when you experience one of these, you know in your inner man that God is trying to tell you something. Nevertheless, it's up to you to pay attention and seek out the meaning through biblical interpretation.

If you would like more information on visions and being caught up in the Spirit, you can start by reading about Paul's vision (beginning at 2 Corinthians 12:2), Cornelius's vision (beginning at Acts 10:3), and Peter's vision (beginning at Acts 10:10). There are many more wonderful dreams, visions and encounters throughout the Bible where God meets with His beloved creation.

As I close out this chapter, I must say that I didn't completely understand what my vision meant at that time. Although I knew in my heart that God had a very good reason for visiting us in such an extraordinary way. I also perceived He was trying to show us something that was coming soon.

What is mankind that you are mindful of them, human beings that you care for them? (Psalms 8:4).

In all reality, is anyone really worthy of such an honor? I'm certainly no one special, and my family isn't either. Nevertheless, the God I love and serve daily came to me and showed me the wonder of His love.

But why? And why me?

Who am I that the God of the universe would come to me in such a majestic and glorious way, or even be mindful of me at all? Although, when you think about it, if being worthy was a prerequisite, no one throughout all of time would have such a glorious honor as that.

As Oswald Chambers reminds us in *My Utmost for His Highest*, we don't know when He will touch us, but oh how awesome it is when he does.

3

God's Purpose for the Vision

"For I know the plans I have for you," declares the LORD
(Jeremiah 29:11).

As I said before, I didn't completely understand the reason for my vision or its meaning at the time it was given. Nonetheless, I knew God was up to something, and I couldn't wait to see what it was. Words can't express how extremely thankful I was to have experienced something so incredible. The next few months were like walking on clouds. I could have lived on that mountaintop and the memory of it for the rest of my life. I couldn't stop wondering, why had He come to us in such an incredible way? Where was this place he was leading us?

Over time, I came to understand that our mountaintop moments are meant for inspiration and perhaps even insight—the valleys are where we prove ourselves. Where our faithfulness to God is revealed.

So allow me to take you down from my mountaintop, like Jesus did with His disciples, into the valley below, where the vision and the purpose for the vision will be explained.

In Matthew 17:1-13, Jesus took His three closest disciples, John, James, and Peter, to the top of a mountain. There they saw the glorious transfiguration of their Lord before He led them back down into the valley below—the place where the vision would be better understood.

As I said before, after my mountaintop encounter with Jesus, I thought He was preparing me for something wonderful and exciting. I felt privileged to have had such an amazing encounter, and I couldn't wait to see what it was all about. As you will see, God did indeed have a profound purpose in giving me that experience, but my expectations of glorious days just up ahead could not have been more wrong.

Instead, He was preparing me to die. Yes, die! Die to everything that would keep me from fulfilling my God-given destiny and purpose for being here.

Jesus said, Very truly I tell you, unless a kernel of wheat falls to the ground and dies, it remains only a single seed. But if it dies, it produces many seeds (John 12:24). Without knowing it at the time, I was about to embark on what would become a ten-year journey through the darkest and most difficult time of my life. Nevertheless, throughout that journey, the memory of my encounter with the Lord kept me going, even though they were my darkest days. Looking back, I now understand why I needed to die to myself and everything that was not of Him. Yes, Jesus came to me in such an unforgettable way for two reasons. First, He wanted me to know without a shadow of doubt the depth of His unconditional love for me. Jesus knew that if I understood that, I would never have to ask, "God, why are You allowing this to happen to me?" Or to ask, "Don't You love me?" Knowing Jesus was right there with me, holding my hand, and knowing the reality of His love not only kept me going during my darkest days, but it helped me to remain in control of my fears, emotions, and doubts.

Second, He wanted me to know that there was a greater purpose for my pain. (I believe writing this book to help others was a big part of that purpose.) By the end of my journey, I had died to the weak, fearful woman I once was and become the fearless warrior He destined me to be. Yes, I had become fearless in the face of the enemy and extremely bold in whatever it was that Jesus wanted me to do. Looking back now, I can see clearly that He was preparing me and my boys for something wonderful and exciting all right, but there was still much work to be done in all of our lives to prepare us for God's *greater* purpose and destiny.

Little did I realize as I was making my slow and joyful descent down the mountain and into the valley below, my hopes and dreams of a perfect life with godly children would soon be challenged beyond what I could possibly imagine. I never thought they would trade their love for the true and living God for the counterfeit that Satan offers in the world. However, only seven months later, that "perfect," hope-filled world started to shake when the first dark and ominous clouds of my storm appeared. Suddenly, and without warning, it felt like I was thrown down into a dark, demon-possessed valley.

While seeking a word of hope and encouragement from the Lord one day, I opened my daily devotional by Oswald Chambers, *My Utmost for His Highest*, and found a profound description that perfectly explained my vision on the mount with Jesus and the deep drudgery I was now facing in the valley below. There, on the page, he had described my life at that exact time. What I hadn't understood, and what Chambers made clear, was that whatever God was preparing me for on the mountaintop couldn't be learned or explained up there. Like the disciples, only in the valley of the shadow of death and deep darkness could I learn to walk out my faith and live for the glory of the Lord. It was during this time down in the valley that my faith—like the disciples'—would be tested for all it was worth.

The meaning of my vision was about to play out in all of our lives, and it would soon be time to prove my spiritual resolve. If the height of the mountaintop is measured by the drudgery of the demon-filled valley, then I must have gone into the bowels of hell. Nevertheless, it was in this place of humiliation and heartache that we all found our true worth to God as our faithfulness was revealed. Yes, soon we would all learn to live in the valley according to our own personal relationship with Him. No longer could our sons count on our strong personal relationship with God to get them through this valley. They were both forced to develop their own deep and personal relationship with the Lord. One thing was for certain, if there was any skepticism left in our hearts after the vision, this dismal valley was sure to drive it out. I could believe that anything was possible while on the mountaintop with Jesus, but now that I was in total darkness, could I still believe that He alone held all the power in heaven and on earth? Could He make the absolutely impossible, possible?

Now that I'd been plunged into the deep, dark waters of the raging river in the valley below, I would for the first time in my life experience a level of heartache and humiliation I never knew possible. To add insult to injury, it would be played out on a stage called Charlotte's Life . . . for everyone to see.

What would my once fiery faith look like now while the world was watching? Would I run and hide like all my emotions wanted me to? Because, to be honest, that's really what I felt like doing. I was flooded with a medley of emotions and unanswered questions that I was forced to face as reality began to set in. Would I try to hide it and keep everything shrouded in darkness? Let's face it, I had just received a big fat F on my parental report card. And I knew the enemy wanted me to never speak of it again to anyone, let alone use my story to help others and see them set free from this prison cell.

I was in the valley of decision . . . what would I do with my new failing grade? The answer came straight from my heart, and I knew exactly what to do. I was going to tell my feelings to stand down to the Spirit of the Living God and take on His emotions instead, and rise up standing tall with my head held high, believing and trusting that the Lord was still at my right hand, even though I could no longer see Him?

Let your face shine on your servant; save me in your unfailing love. Let me not be put to shame . . . In the shelter of your presence you hide them from all human intrigues; you keep them safe in your dwelling from accusing tongues (Psalm 31:16,17,20).

I wasn't going to worry about what people would say about me, and I wasn't going to become a skillful skeptic and live in a place called Defeat. Oh no, my mind was set, and I was determined that I was not going to become another victim of the enemy, a witness like so many others who had stood helplessly by while the enemy devoured their child. Nevertheless, I must admit, I wasn't prepared for the grip of the evil one's debilitating fear, as he tried to keep me down and consume my very soul. Some days it seemed that no matter how desperately I tried to get up and keep moving forward, this spirit of fear would shove me back down again. Oh, but I was determined to rise up out of this valley of suffering and misery like a mighty warrior of the true and living God. I knew the Lord was still holding on to my right hand, and I was determined to take hold of the purpose for which He had taken hold of me!

The LORD is with me like a mighty warrior (Jeremiah 20:11).

The truth is, the choices were mine. God wasn't going to make me fight back, and He certainly couldn't keep me in the battle if I wasn't willing to fight. The choice was completely up to me.

But if I say, "I will not mention his word or speak anymore in his name," his word is in my heart like a fire, a fire shut up in my bones (Jeremiah 20:9).

My friend, the dark, demon-filled valley is the place where everything you have practiced and believed as a Christian will be challenged beyond your wildest imagination. In other words, it will be a defining moment in your life! Every day from this moment on will depend on the decisions you make in your own Garden of Gethsemane.

Like Jesus when He made up His mind in the Garden of Gethsemane to go to the cross for our sins no matter what lay ahead, we too will have to decide. After that decision was made, there was no turning back for Him. He knew what He came for . . . to die!

Now your time has come to die!

God is asking you if you are willing to make that same decision for your child's life too . . . no matter what, even unto death. You must decide. There's no turning back once that decision is made. Your heart is set on victory, just like Jesus' was.

Once you've made the choice to enter the fight, you will need deep-water faith to reach the other side. Trust me, like I said before, there's no room for shallow Christian faith when you've been thrown into the deep end. Ready or not, you're there. And there's only one way out—you must swim through it until you reach the other side. And the reality is, you didn't even swim out there by your own will to begin with—you were thrown out there because of someone you loved dearly. Things get more unsettling when you realize it's your faithful Father God who has *allowed* you to be thrown into the deep and raging waters.

But why?

Could it be that He chose you for this assignment before He formed you in your mother's womb? Perhaps He knew you would be His secret weapon to defeat the enemy with all along? Did God know when He gave you this particular child that this day would come? Absolutely He did! And that's why He chose you to be their parent. He made sure everything you needed to defeat this giant and win the war was already inside of you, placed there by His divine hand even before you were born. *Before I formed you in the womb I knew you, before you were born I set you apart; I appointed you...* (Jeremiah 1:5)

Yes, He knew that you would pass through this raging storm, therefore, He knitted you together perfectly and set you apart for this divine purpose. The Lord says, *When you pass through the waters, I will be with you; and when you pass through the rivers, they will not sweep over you. When you walk through the fire, you will not be burned; the flames will not set you ablaze. For I am the Lord your God, the Holy One of Israel, your Savior* (Isaiah 43:2-3).

He will be with you. You need to know that! And He's getting ready to show you what He placed inside of you that you have no idea is already there. Trust me when I say, if God brought you to this dark valley, He has already given you everything you will need to get *through* it. Oh yes, He hardwired you for this assignment while knitting you together in your mother's womb. Yes, my friend, He will be faithful to bring you safely to the other side! But here's *the secret*: you must keep your eyes on Him continually! And all the while, Satan and his demon warriors will be trying to distract you with the wind and waves of the storm. At times, those stormy seas will get so rough it will feel like the boat is about to be tossed upside down and into certain destruction at any moment. And if you haven't yet learned how to swim, spiritually speaking, then this training will be the most difficult thing you have ever gone through in your entire life.

First, you must learn how to swim, or at least tread water until you can swim. You're probably asking yourself, *How will I ever do this with so much destruction going on, not to mention the whirlwind of emotions swirling around me?*

You will do it by remembering the secret: by keeping your eyes fastened on Him for swimming instructions (battle instructions) at all times.

God is your only true life preserver out in the deep, so whatever you do, don't let go or lose sight of your preserver! Don't let Him out of your sight . . . no matter what the enemy does! Remember my life scripture verse, from Matthew 6:33? Seek Him first!

Again, I promise you He will be faithful to teach you how to swim safely to the other side. You won't drown if you will just keep your eyes fastened on Him and follow His lead.

When my faith was challenged and tested beyond anything I had ever experienced in my Christian walk, I discovered quickly that I wasn't the strong swimmer I thought I was. Even so, Jesus went down into that deep water with me and gave me daily swimming lessons. On my weakest days, when my strength was completely gone, He went down into the deep and carried me through the stormy waters. On other weary days, He brought a few brave lifelines—people who noticed I was struggling. Yes, they went out into the deep too, and encouraged my weary soul through prayer. Eventually, with many trials and tribulations, I learned how to be a strong and powerful swimmer like Him. The process could have gone much faster, but I often got in the way. Why? Because I wasn't as spiritually fit as I thought I was, nor was I as disciplined as I needed to be. I would get weary in the battle and rest when I should have been doing my strength training—reading the Bible and staying devoted to prayer. But I knew God did not give me a *spirit of slavery to fall back into fear* (Romans 8:15 ESV). Oh no, I had *received the Spirit of adoption as sons, by whom we cry "Abba! Father!"* (verse 15 continued). *He said to me, "You are my son; today I have become your Father. Ask me . . .* (Psalm 2:7-8).

Papa God knew there was much work to be done all right, especially in the early days. Slowly but surely though, with His persistent nudging, I caught on to the all-important need for self-discipline and active participation. As I put these two powerful principles into action, my faith became stronger. Before long, my spiritual muscles developed, and they eventually became so strong that I was able to swim with Him by my side out into the deepest waters—where the current was the strongest. You see, my friend, living in the spirit aligns you with the mind of Christ. As sons of God, we are more than conquerors.

Now my friend, it's time for you to prove *your* spiritual resolve— your spiritual grit!

As I said before, if you have never learned to swim (spiritually speaking) this will be an extremely tough time of training. But if you will remember to always put God and His righteous ways at the forefront of all you do, in due season the victory will be declared in your favor!

Remember, our God has never lost a war! He always has a strategy and a battle plan! He specializes in teaching us how to become strong and courageous Olympic-level swimmers. He's not taken back by our weakness, because it's in our weakness that He makes us strong.

But he said to me, "My grace is sufficient for you, for my power is made perfect in weakness." Therefore I will boast all the more gladly about my weaknesses, so that Christ's power may rest on me. That is why, for Christ's sake, I delight in weaknesses, in insults, in hardships, in persecutions, in difficulties. For when I am weak, then I am strong (2 Corinthians 12:9-10).

Yes, when we're at our weakest state, it's during this time that He proves through us who He is, as others witness our courageous, unrelenting faith in Him. As the world looks on, they will see you accomplish the impossible and know it was your amazing God—the One you boasted about all through the trial—who gave you your great victory!

Yes, God is faithful, and He will teach you how to be a bold and courageous warrior, filled with His Holy Power and valor. Believe it or not, by the time you complete this journey, you will be fearless in the face of your enemy. Trust me when Is tell you, I didn't come out of the valley looking the same way I did when I went in!

Again, I promise you, if you will put God first place in every area of your life and stay in the fight, He will teach you how to swim with Him in the raging current. Then He will use the *same* raging current to take you to where He wants you to go—straight to your and your prodigal child's purpose and destiny.

Yes, His perfect will and destiny for all of you will be found out in the deepest waters—so start swimming!

4

The Call to Battle

Therefore let everyone who is godly offer prayer to you
at a time when you may be found; surely in the rush of great waters,
they shall not reach him (Psalm 32:6 ESV).

I know you are ready to get right into the battle instruction, but let me briefly give you a little background about my oldest son first. This will give you a better understanding later on in the story of why the enemy of my soul was so determined to destroy this young man. And it may help you understand why he is so determined to do the same thing to your child.

The story of my young warrior son started with a simple prayer request when I was only two months pregnant. This was my prayer: "Lord, I'm asking You for a son so that he may one day be used as a minister of God."

Immediately in my mind, I heard the Lord laugh. And then He said, "You will have a son."

The One enthroned in heaven laughs (Psalm 2:4).

I had never before, nor have I since, heard the Lord laugh. But I heard it then. It was the sweetest laugh—almost a chuckle. And, interestingly enough, it wouldn't be the last time God was heard laughing about this child. But more on that to come.

From that time on, I refused to be told my baby's sex. I made it clear to the medical staff at my ultrasound appointments that I didn't want them to tell me. Whenever someone would ask what I was having, I would say, by faith, "Between me and the Lord, it's a boy."

When the day came, I gave birth to a handsome little baby boy who I knew would someday be used as a mighty warrior of God. And while all mothers are partial to their children, he was everything a mother could ever ask for in a son. He was handsome, joyful, and he had a rollicking sense of humor. But, most importantly, he had an amazing sensitivity to the presence of God's Spirit, even at a very early age.

At the age of two, while we were gathered around the dinner table one evening, my son announced, "I want Jesus in my heart." He was always announcing things, but we weren't even talking about Jesus at the time, nor had we been earlier that day. It was completely inspired by the Holy Spirit, and we all knew it. I looked at him and said, "Okay, little buddy, tonight at bedtime, we will ask Jesus to come live in your heart."

That night I carefully explained God's plan of salvation to him on a simple, toddler's level. I slowly recited the sinner's prayer, and he repeated each phrase after me and asked Jesus to come live in his heart. I remember basking in the moment and then thinking how amazing it was that he had such a sensitivity to the Holy Spirit at such a young age. I mean, he was barely two years old!

At age three, he made the same announcement. Once again, I talked to him about what that meant and the importance of Jesus living in his heart and I led him once again in prayer.

Many years later, as we went through the most difficult years with him, God told me something I will never forget. He said, "I selected you, daughter, to be his mother. I could have given him to anyone, but I chose you, because I knew I could trust you to teach him My ways. Because My Spirit lives in him, I will always lead him back to Me throughout his life."

I can't tell you how comforting it was to hear those words. Yes, God knew my child even before He formed him in my womb, and He had placed that much trust in me. I must say, I was determined that His trust and confidence would not be lost on me!

Before I formed you in the womb I knew you (Jeremiah 1:5).

You see, I was radically saved only two years before my son was born, while I was pregnant with my daughter, and, believe me, I wanted to shout it from the rooftops! During those two years before his birth, I regularly attended a local church, but it always seemed like there was something missing. Then, right before my son was born, the Air Force moved us to Indiana. I desperately wanted to find a great church, but after visiting several, I still hadn't found the right one. I was discouraged. To be honest, I couldn't feel His presence in any of them. (If you don't feel God's presence in a church, why would you stay there? If He's moved on and His glory has departed from that place, perhaps you should move on too, and find a place where His glory dwells.)

So one morning, after praying the night before for God's leading, I was led by the Spirit to a church in another town twenty minutes away. In my mind, I could actually see what the church sign looked like, but I couldn't see any letters on the sign, only the shape of it and the colors. The pole was white and big and round. The sign was rectangular with a royal-blue border and white background. After twenty minutes of driving, I started to think I had made that sign up in my head. Then, there it was! I couldn't wait to get inside and see what God had in store for me. And sure enough, I wasn't disappointed as I walked in and felt His wonderful presence.

After I'd attended only a few weeks, they offered an opportunity for anyone in the church to learn to share the gospel. I jumped at the opportunity and soon became a soul-winning machine. For the next eight years, I was involved in a weekly ministry on Tuesday nights, visiting the homes of people who had visited our church.

Sharing the gospel became a way of life for me. Only God knows how many people I led to the Lord during that time, because I lost count after a while. My husband, Steve, was the first person I ever led to the Lord. What a great start, Lord! Oh yes, I was finally given a chance to shout it from the rooftops all right. And that I did!

Meanwhile, we were raising our children for Christ, and to the best of our ability we were living holy lives inside and outside our home. We all loved Jesus. I had made many sacrifices to stay at home with my kids throughout their childhood and right on through the teenage years. Steve and I were completely involved in their lives, from coaching baseball games to school fieldtrips and everything in between. I even worked within the youth ministry with my own little ministry while the kids were in youth group. During this time, I would take all of the first-time visitors and the friends who invited them to my little ministry room, give them pizza, and share about our amazing youth group, and then share my testimony. After that, I would share the gospel with anyone who wanted to stay behind. I can't tell you how many youths I led to Jesus during those years either, but there were many weeks that the entire room came to know Christ. As you can probably tell by now, winning souls was (and still is) my passion!

Before long, the youth pastor and I were leading kids to Christ week after week, the once small youth group was starting to grow. Soon after that, we had a very large youth group that was still growing. Then, one day during one of our many conversations, our extremely anointed youth pastor said something to me that I'll never forget. He said, "The Devil will let you have a few kids, but when you start to impact the kingdom of darkness, he will take notice of you."

It wasn't long after hearing the youth pastor say those words that I heard the Devil say, *I'm going to wipe that smile right off your face*, as I shared with you earlier.

That night, I knew in my heart, trouble was on the way.

You see, if there was one thing Satan hated most about me, probably just as much as he hated me stealing souls, it was the fullness of God's joy in my heart. I was always smiling and laughing, and I know

Satan hated the sound of my joyful voice.

Soon after hearing those ominous words, I went to a prayer meeting, where I knew a true prophetess of the Lord would be speaking. My full intent was to have her pray and prophesy over my son. He was sixteen at this time, and I'd already noticed that his heart was being led away from God. Therefore, as the Lord instructed me, I took a photo of him to the meeting for her to pray over.

As the prophetess spoke to me, she took the photo in her hand and started to pray for him. Not long after she started praying, she stopped, looked at me, and said, "I hear the Lord laughing!" I smiled and shook my head as to say, yes! Then, with a puzzled look on her face, she asked, "Why is the Lord laughing?" I said, "I don't know, but I heard Him laugh, too, the day I asked Him for a son that would be used as a minister."

At that moment, we both burst out in laughter! This was the first time she'd ever heard the Lord laugh. Interestingly enough, the Lord didn't reveal to her what He was laughing about either. This mystery would remain hidden until the appointed time.

It seems as though God loves to do things in secret. Just like any loving parent, He loves to surprise His children with good things. At the perfect time, He surprises them with something that goes above and beyond anything they could ever think, hope, or imagine! So don't give up, my friend, because God has a glorious surprise in store for you, one that's going to blow your mind!

Now to Him who is able to do exceedingly abundantly above all that we ask or think, according to the power that works in us, to Him be glory (Ephesians 3:20-21 NKJV).

***

And sure enough, only a few years after that vicious threat, the war began.

Our dark and dreadful journey started with my entire family

gathered at the local Outback Steakhouse. On that day every year, we celebrate three birthdays at once, because they're so close together. My oldest son's is one of those three. And this particular day, everyone was there—the entire family, grandparents included.

Everyone except my son.

At first, we thought he was running a little late and would arrive at any minute. As the evening went on and he didn't call or show up, I remember thinking, *something really bad has happened.* I knew he wouldn't miss our ritual birthday celebration unless something was keeping him from being there.

When he never showed up, we started to look for him. We called his friends, but no one knew where he was. Then we called the police. To our shock, we learned he was in jail.

Not knowing what God would have us do, we decided to leave him there overnight. Early the next morning, while seeking direction for my son from the Lord in prayer, the Lord spoke to my heart and said, "Leave him in there for three days and three nights. As Jonah was in the belly of the whale for three days and three nights, so will your son be in jail."

Meanwhile, my husband was already up and getting ready to go get him out. When he came into my prayer room, I told him what the Lord told me we should do. I'm not sure if he didn't believe I'd heard clearly from the Lord or if he just couldn't bear the thought of leaving his son in jail for two more nights. Either way, he disregarded what I said and went to get him out. Of course, I didn't try to stop him or push the matter at that point because, truth was, I couldn't stand the thought of leaving him in there either.

This was all new to us. We had never experienced anyone in our family going to jail before. We were standing at a new door so to speak. God was faithful as always, and He was trying to tell us what to do, but we couldn't receive His instruction and follow through because our faith wasn't as strong as we thought. Unfortunately, that day marked the beginning of a ten-year journey filled with much regret, not to mention deep sorrow and suffering.

We've both often wondered what would have happened if we'd slowed down to confirm what the Lord had spoken to us that morning and obeyed Him. We were mature Christian believers, and we knew in our hearts that God really could do what needed to be done in our son's heart in only three days and three nights. However, our disobedience—and our son's disobedience—proved to be one of the biggest mistakes of our lives. The consequences of our disobedience would play out over the coming years, and all of us would suffer those consequences together.

Matthew 12:40 says, *For as Jonah was three days and three nights in the belly of a huge fish, so the Son of Man will be three days and three nights in the heart of the earth.* You can see from this passage that Jonah was in a place that felt like hell with no way out, and Jesus compared His own trip to hell (after his death) to this same story. Little did we know, we too were about to enter into the depths of hell! Although we didn't see it at the time, God saw that our son was walking away from his faith and dying spiritually. He allowed our son to go to jail (into the belly of the whale) to show him some things he could not see any other way. I now believe that in those three days and three nights, God would have raised his dying soul back from the dead and given him back his life.

We must learn to trust God and let Him get our kids where He wants them to be—not where we want them to be. Jesus said, Why do you call me, *'Lord, Lord,' and do not do what I say? As for everyone who comes to me and hears my words and puts them into practice, I will show you what they are like. They are like a man building a house, who dug down deep and laid the foundation on rock. When a flood came, the torrent struck that house but could not shake it, because it was well built* (Luke 6:46).

As we can see from the words of our Savior, if He is Lord of our lives, then we need to do what He tells us to do. You see, that first time in jail was just for a small violation. It didn't cost anything to get him out—only his father's signature. But our son would be sent to jail again, and the next time wouldn't be so easy.

***

I once read a very interesting book about the courtroom of heaven. I'm not sure, but from what I read, I now believe Satan could have been building his case against my son in God's courtroom. But God was trying to overturn the verdict by reasoning with our son in jail and bringing him to a place of repentance. As we can see from reading the Bible and looking at acts of willful sin in people's lives, willful sin gives the Devil *opportunity*. Also, when left uncheck, it gives the enemy a foothold or a right to attack us as we cross over into his territory and remain there. That's why God's Word warns us: *Do not give the devil a foothold* (Ephesians 4:27). Also, it says, *And do not grieve the Holy Spirit of God, with whom you were sealed for the day of redemption* (Ephesians 4:30).

Only when there is true repentance can justification take place. Jesus died that we may be justified (or made right with God). Jesus is our justification. Without this true repentance, or turning away from willful sin, we inadvertently give Satan a right to come back into our lives and try to destroy us. And I believe from what the Scriptures tell us, our loving God will allow this to happen, if necessary, to bring us back to a place of true repentance.

I truly believe that whatever God wanted to do in our son's heart would have taken the same amount of time it took Jonah to repent and obey God's will for his life if he would have spent that time in jail. When Jonah came out of the whale's belly, he not only asked God's forgiveness, but he truly repented for his sin of disobedience by obeying God and following God's instructions to the letter. May we never forget that true freedom over sin comes through sincere repentance. Playing games with our salvation is always dangerous!

Looking back, I know God had something prepared for our son in that jail cell. Something He could have and *would* have accomplished in only three days and three nights. But our quick decision and lack of trust shut the door on what He wanted to do, and inadvertently opened it wide for the enemy and his demons to come in and do what *they* wanted to do. Yes, we were left to face the fallout and the destruction that was sure to follow because of our disobedience to His divine instructions.

One very important thing I have learned from this journey: everything in a Christian's life rests on obedience. I truly believe that obedience unlocks the activity of God in a believer's life. In the same way, disobedience and willful sin unlocks satanic activity and gives Satan freedom to come in.

Both my husband and I now know that God wanted to use our son's jail time to teach him something in a place where he'd be forced to face the reality of his disobedience. The Bible says in Proverbs 3:5, *Trust in the Lord with all thine heart; and lean not unto thine own understanding* (KJV). However, we decided to lean on our own understanding and be led by our fearful emotions. Not only did we rush out ahead of God, we didn't even take the time to pray together and seek the Lord to confirm that it was His will. We learned a horrible and painful lesson from that hasty decision.

The Word of God also says in Proverbs 14:12, *There is a way that appears to be right, but in the end it leads to death.*

But then, hindsight is 20/20.

Interestingly enough, by getting our son out of jail so quickly, it soon felt like we had set in motion the story of Jonah in *all* our lives.

***

You see, like Jonah, our son was on the run from God's will for his life. And just like those poor souls who were in the boat with Jonah were affected by his actions, my husband and I were also in the boat together with our son. Much like their story, the storm grew stronger and stronger, and, like most loving parents, we tried desperately not to throw our son overboard. We prayed, we tried reasoning with him, we did everything we could think of to calm the storm. We were bailing water from the boat and rowing those oars as hard as we could. But the raging storm kept on belting us with the waves and wind. Finally, in our weariness, when we had no more strength left to fight, we surrendered to the will and plan of God for his life . . . we threw him overboard.

Yes, we kicked our son out of our home. The waters seemed to still for a moment but, in reality, our hearts went overboard with him that day. Making that decision was one of the hardest decisions we ever had to make. In our hearts, we knew it was time to let go of him and trust God, but it literally felt like we'd thrown him into the raging sea.

Although our son was over the age of eighteen at this time, I'm not telling you to follow the exact instructions the Lord gave us. I'm telling you our story to encourage you to take some time in prayer before you act. Wait on the Lord and get a word of confirmation from Him. Put out a fleece if you need to, but wait for God's wise counsel.

David the Psalmist said, *Wait for the LORD; be strong and take heart and wait for the LORD.* (Psalm 27:14) Seek Him for His will for your child or loved one. If you aren't a strong Christian, then call a pastor or someone you know who hears clearly from God. Then, by faith, follow the Lord's instructions.

We eventually allowed our son to return home, but the next few months after this were heart wrenching as we watched him struggle between what he knew in his heart was right and the world's enticements. We could see the struggle as Satan used his friends and alcohol to lure him into a life of sin, death, and destruction. We got him back into church, but his heart was no longer where his body was. He had become a captive by choice—his own choice. Before long, he was full on into drinking and partying.

The party scene was always active and alive in our area because we lived only thirty minutes from some of the most beautiful coastal beaches. Unfortunately, we were naïve, and allowed our son to work at the beach during the summers for extra money.

I'm sure my son thought he was in control of his situation and just enjoying the pleasures of this new and exciting life for a season. Knowing him as a mother does, I believe he had no intentions of staying there that long. He knew deep in his heart where he was supposed to be. But as the saying goes, sin will take you further than you ever intended to go, keep you longer than you ever intended to stay, and cost you more than you ever wanted to pay.

The Word of God says, *But each person is tempted when they are dragged away by their own evil desire and enticed* (James 1:14).

One day during this same time, the Lord gave me a word of knowledge for my son. God spoke very clearly to me and told me to read Isaiah 1:18-20: *"Come now, let us settle the matter," says the Lord. "Though your sins are like scarlet, they shall be as white as snow; though they are red as crimson, they shall be like wool. If you are willing and obedient, you will eat the good things of the land; but if you resist and rebel, you will be devoured by the sword." For the mouth of the Lord has spoken.*

When I read that last part—*for the mouth of the Lord has spoken*—it took my breath away. I knew this was a powerful warning to my son from the Lord. After reading the passage, the Lord told me to give this warning to my son.

God was giving him one last chance to stop what he was doing and turn back to Him. So I prayed that my son would heed the warning from the Lord and turn away from the sin in his life before it was too late. I prayed that he would see this as something extremely serious.

After praying, I laid the Bible out on the counter and asked him to come in and read the passage. He seemed to carefully read over the passage, but I wasn't sure if he really took it for the serious warning it was. I explained that the Lord told me to give him the passage as a warning. Then I began to almost beg him to turn from the ways of the world and give his heart and life back to God before it was too late.

I would love to tell you that my son received the wakeup call that he needed just from reading this powerful warning. Unfortunately, he didn't, and that was the last warning he would receive before going to jail for the second time.

Our journey through the dark, demon-possessed valley was about to get darker than we ever imagined. The former darkness we experienced in the sea where we frantically splashed around trying not to drown after going overboard with our son would soon pale in comparison to being swallowed up by a giant whale!

***

Only a few months after this final warning, the "Great Whale" in Jonah's story found us while we were still sinking ever deeper into the dark, stormy waters below the boat. My husband and I stood in shock as we read in the local newspaper that our son had been arrested once again! It felt like a shockwave had just run straight through my body. The same shockwave I'm sure Jonah must have felt after suddenly being swallowed up by a whale. This shockwave was immediately followed by emotions of eminent doom, as debilitating fear seemed to swallow me whole. I will never forget the depth of despair that engulfed my entire being as I read that article.

While this medley of paralyzing emotions seemed to devour my very soul, I can give praise to my faithful God that He made sure two very strong lifelines were right there with me that day. Despite how alone and empty I felt in that petrifying instant, I wasn't actually physically alone. Thank God, my husband and dear friend Lisa, were right there by my side.

Interestingly enough, when this took place, Lisa, my dear friend of over twenty years, had just come over from Mississippi for a couple of days to catch up on old times. Lisa and I were very close friends—she was actually one of the people I led to the Lord back in the early 1980s, right after my 180-degree conversion and learning to share the gospel. You could probably say God had brought the bread of life I needed that day back to me.

Cast your bread on the surface of the waters, for you will find it after many days. (Ecclesiastes 11:1 NASB).

To this day I believe that's why God made sure my friend Lisa was there with me that day. She is probably one of the most anointed encouragers and exhorters I've ever known, not to mention the true sturdy lifeline I needed that day. God used her insightful gift of discernment to bring comfort and clarity to some of the madness. I remember her reading over the article again very carefully. Then she gave an account of what she believed the Lord had shown her, and what actually happened that night that led to my son's arrest. I remember her saying "You wait and see. That's what really happened!"

We would soon discover the real details about what happened on that dreadful night and how the local newspaper had sensationalized the story. Nevertheless, Lisa's insightful account of what she gave believed the Lord had shown her was spot on with my son's side of the story.

Besides, we all know this is what newspaper publishers do to sell newspapers. They intentionally write headlines in a way that will provoke public attention and interest, whether the story is good or bad. Unfortunately, sometimes it's at the expense of accuracy—and others' lives.

Nevertheless, for the first time in our lives we were about to embark on a journey that would stretch our faith to a whole new level. Remember the shallow water faith I was talking about earlier? Well, we were about to see how well that works when you're thrown into the deep end!

5

Can These Dry Bones Live?

I will give you a new heart and put a new spirit in you . . . I will put my Spirit in you and move you to follow my decrees (Ezekiel 36:26-27).

I wish I could say I handled myself well the first time I saw my son in jail, but, the truth is, I didn't at all.

I guess I wasn't prepared to see him in that environment. At the first sight of him, I burst into tears. I couldn't settle myself long enough to listen to what he had to say, although I desperately wanted to hear his side of the story. I knew he was the only one who could make sense of it all.

Thank God my husband was somewhat in control of his emotions and listened carefully as our son gave us a much different account of what happened than the newspaper's version.

The charges brought on our son were serious. Regardless of his side of the story, the fact was that our son was in jail, facing a possible prison sentence.

That said, we didn't want to make the same mistake we'd made before and rush in to have him released. This time we would wait on the Lord and follow His instructions to the letter. In my heart, I knew this test would prove to be one of the most horrendous trials of our Christian faith. And this time, we were determined to trust God explicitly! Therefore as the Lord instructed us, our son remained in jail until the day he was sentenced. It was during this time that my faith—like the disciples'—would be tested for all it was worth.

Yes, it was time to prove our spiritual steadfastness once again.

***

Now the second scene in my vision, which had begun with the mountaintop, had become completely clear. We had been thrust into a valley all right, but by this time we were in a place of deep darkness. I finally understood what I could not see at the time of the vision, when Jesus was holding my hand and leading me through the valley below. Now, in the darkness, I would learn to *keep* holding His hand as I walked by a way that I had never been before. It's during such times that we all learn to walk by faith and not by sight.

For we live by faith, not by sight (2 Corinthians 5:7).

As devastating as it was to face this situation, we were determined not to give up on our son or our God's will for his life. To be completely honest, we would have fought for his well-being until our dying breath. Therefore, we knew it was time to keep moving forward and find a good lawyer for our son.

***

On our way to the attorney's office, the Lord asked me something I'll never forget. He spoke right into my mind and said, *Can these dry bones live?*

I was familiar with the Bible passage those words came from and I was pretty sure it was in Ezekiel somewhere. As I pondered the meaning and tried to understand what He was asking, He asked me the same question again.

Can these dry bones live?

I remembered my pastor saying, when the Lord is trying to tell you something important, He will repeat it, so I knew to pay close attention when He said it the second time. This time when He asked me again, I remembered how Ezekiel responded to the Lord's question, and said, *". . . LORD, you alone know"* (Ezekiel 37:3).

By the time we got to the lawyer's office, I knew God was up to something—something amazing, and I couldn't wait to see what He was trying to tell me.

When I finally got my hands on a Bible, I went straight to the book of Ezekiel. It literally fell open to the exact passage I remembered:

The hand of the Lord was on me, and he brought me out by the Spirit of the Lord and set me in the middle of a valley; it was full of bones. He led me back and forth among them, and I saw a great many bones on the floor of the valley, bones that were very dry. He asked me, "Son of man, can these bones live?" I said, "Sovereign Lord, you alone know" (Ezekiel 37:1-3).

You may be asking what in the world that means. Well, when the Lord first asked me that question, I wasn't sure either. But after reading all of Ezekiel 37, I had a pretty good idea of what it meant and why we were in this dreary valley of dead, dry bones. But most importantly, I knew what God was trying to do in my son's life. And I also had my new battle instructions! My marching orders were very clear. The symbolism here and how it relates to my son's story is amazing . . .

The dry bones in the valley (like the valley we were living in now) represented God's chosen people, the Israelites. They, like my son, had rebelled against God, doing exactly what He warned them not to do. The warning appears in Isaiah 1:18, which, if you remember, is the warning I gave my son before he ended up in jail. The one he too failed to heed.

Like my son, the Lord allowed Israel to go into captivity. I say *allowed* because God could have stopped it. But the Israelites (like my son) were dying spiritually because of their willful sinning against God and because they were doing *what God had told them not to do.*

Keep in mind, the Bible says: *The Lord disciplines those he loves, as a father the son he delights in* (Proverbs 3:12). This was a time of disciplining for the Israelites, the children God dearly loved. They too were warned, but would not listen to God the gentler way. And because my son would not listen the gentler way either, even though he was warned with the same warning God gave the Israelites, this was a time of harsh discipline for him. However, with that disciplining, God was asking me to trust Him and believe that He would do in my son's life what He promised to do in the life of His Israelite children. And that was to bring him back to life again and make him into a great warrior of God.

Spiritually speaking, my son's life was as good as dead. He was like the dead, dry bones on the valley floor. But God, in His great mercy, did not take my son's life from him. Instead, He took him away from the world he was living in and put him somewhere else—*jail* (captivity). He did this in order to force him to see how far he'd wandered away from Him, and to use that time to bring him back.

We see this in Ezekiel 36:24, where God says, *I will take you out of the nations*. God took the Israelites out of the nations that were sinful and allowed them to go into captivity. The passage continues in verse 25 where the Lord said to Ezekiel:

I will sprinkle clean water on you, and you will be clean; I will cleanse you from all your impurities and from all your idols. I will give you a new heart and put a new spirit in you; I will remove from you your heart of stone and give you a heart of flesh. And I will put my Spirit in you and move you to follow my decrees and be careful to keep my laws. Then you will live in the land I gave your ancestors; you will be my people, and I will be your God (Ezekiel 36:25-28).

God is merciful and doesn't want to punish us. The Word of God says, The LORD is slow to anger, abounding in love and forgiving sin and rebellion. Yet he does not leave the guilty unpunished (Numbers 14:18).

My son's heart had become cold and hard. He no longer wanted to listen to what God had to say because the world and all it had to offer had become his new god. Just like the Israelites had chased after other gods.

But now, in captivity, God had my son's full attention, just like the

Israelites'. He began seeking the Lord as they did, with his whole heart through prayer and the reading of God's Word. My son knew the truth, and he knew how to find his way back to God. And God knew in His infinite wisdom that this was the only way to save him from the world. God was using this time in captivity to develop a godly character in him, because God knew that without it there would be no power in his witness.

May we never forget that without godly character, our witness has no power! Not only that, we will be of little use to God. As a matter of fact, when our character is lacking, we can actually become a stumbling block to others.

Remember when I told you that God made me some promises, and that, by faith, I believed they would come to pass? The amazing promise in Ezekiel 36:25 was my spoken promise from the Lord that day, and trust me when I say, I was determined to follow God's marching orders until the day I saw a warrior arise up out of that valley! From that moment on, I was relentless as I followed God's leading and did what I was instructed. There was no stopping or slowing down until I saw the fullness of my promise come to pass . . . a mighty warrior of God rising up in that young man. As time went on, I could see how God was using this time to cleanse my son's heart by washing him in His clean pure water—God's Word.

Jesus is the fountain of living water that cleanses us from all sin. Jesus said: *But whoever drinks the water I give them will never thirst. Indeed, the water I give them will become in them a spring of water welling up to eternal life* (John 4:14). The Word of God goes on to say, *Whoever believes in me, as the Scripture has said, "Out of his heart will flow rivers of living water"* (John 7:37).

Oh yes, I believed with all my heart that one day I would see those rivers of living water flow out of my son's heart. Jesus is the Word and He is the living water of life; as we live our lives for Him, His life flows out of us like living water by the power of the Holy Spirit. If we will get our hearts right with God by repenting of our sins and asking His forgiveness, we will unstop the dam of willful sin that is keeping the river from flowing in our lives. God is using the dark valley times to dig us up out of our sin filled graves and get all of the dirt off of us. It's His river of living water that cleanses us from all unrighteousness and makes us holy like Him once again. The Word of God says, *But just as he who called you is holy, so be holy in all you do; for it is written: "Be holy, because I am holy"* (1 Peter 1:16).

We can see from reading this scripture, God has set His standard, and it is not the same as this world's standard—oh no! It's a standard of excellence—an excellence that will honor Him in every area of our lives. God expects his children to live holy lives as a reflection of who He is. Just as we can see our own reflection in water, God is transfiguring that reflection as He pours His living water through us. By doing this, God is trying to bring us into a oneness with Him . . . the same oneness that He shared with His Son Jesus. The bottom line is this: He's trying to transfigure our lives and make us a reflection of Him. When people see us, they can't help but see Him in us. That's who the true sons of the Living God look like!

The Word says, *For the anxious longing of the creation waits eagerly for the revealing of the sons of God* (Romans 8:19 NASB).

Who are these sons of God that all of creation is waiting eagerly to be revealed? They are those who have washed their sin-stained robes in the blood of Jesus and become holy. They have passed through the sanctification process and developed His godly character, making themselves useful for God's purposes. The Scriptures explain that they are the true and faithful followers, the ones the Lord calls His "glorious ones," in whom He delights.

As for the saints who are in the land, they are the glorious ones in whom is all my delight (Psalm 16:3).

I took this verse as another promise that God was redeeming the time by making my son into a son of God—one of His glorious ones!

Without a doubt, God was at work, and He was doing His part! Now I had to ask myself, *What is my part to play as his earthly mother in helping him get to that glorious place?*

As I continued to read on in Ezekiel chapter 37, I became very excited and even more hopeful as the answer to that question became very clear in verse four. God tells Ezekiel what He wants him to do to those dead, dry bones.

It was the spiritual strategy I had been waiting for, the marching orders I told you about earlier. . .

Then he said to me, "Prophesy to these bones and say to them, 'Dry bones, hear the word of the Lord! This is what the Sovereign Lord says to these bones: I will make breath[a] enter you, and you will come to life. I will attach tendons to you and make flesh come upon you and cover you with skin; I will put breath in you, and you will come to life. Then you will know that I am the Lord.'"
So I prophesied as I was commanded. And as I was prophesying, there was a noise, a rattling sound, and the bones came together, bone to bone. I looked, and tendons and flesh appeared on them and skin covered them, but there was no breath in them. Then he said to me, "Prophesy to the breath; prophesy, son of man, and say to it, 'This is what the Sovereign Lord says: Come, breath, from the four winds and breathe into these slain, that they may live.'"
So I prophesied as he commanded me, and breath entered them; they came to life and stood up on their feet—a vast army (Ezekiel 37:4-10).

Yes! The dry bones came back to life!

They became a vast army of godly warriors who had learned to stand on their own two feet. With new hearts—godly, soft hearts—that were no longer hardened, but ready to do His will.

When I read those verses, I was overwhelmed with excitement and hope—it was the spiritual strategy I had been waiting for! I knew what the Lord was telling me to do: It was time for me to prophesy! It was time to do as Ezekiel did and speak the word of the Lord over my child by faith, believing that God would do with him what He did with His

Israelite children. Believe me when I say, He will surely do what He says He will do! Why? Because He loves our children . . . they are His children too!

This is what the Lord says—your Redeemer, who formed you in the womb: I am the Lord . . . who carries out the words of his servants and fulfills the predictions of his messengers (Isaiah 44:24-26).

Our God speaks and calls things into existence! *He carries out the words of his servants. He is the God who gives life to the dead and calls into being that which does not exist* (Romans 4:17 AMP).

Now, we see Him telling his servant Ezekiel to do the same thing. To prophesy to dead, dry bones and call life back into them. Not only that, as I read this, I realized this was what He was telling me to do too! After reading these powerful God-breathed instructions, I had my holy orders and His perfect strategic battle plans in my hand. Therefore, as the Lord instructed me, I wrote down a list of all the things in my son's life that had died, and all of my dreams for him that looked as good as dead too. Next, I went on a search for a recent photo of my son. I looked until I found one that made me smile when I looked at it. I took that photo and taped it to the top of my list. Then, while in prayer for him, I called forth these dead things by prophesying to them right out loud. I called each one (just like Ezekiel did by faith) and commanded them to come forth and hear the Word of the Lord!

I was like a kid in a candy store as I wrote down all my dreams and prophecies. Below you will find my personal list of prophecies for my son. I used the biblical word and God's promises as I prophesied His word over my son. I have added this list of prophecies to not only let you see how God answered each one, but to help you get a vision of how to apply biblical promises to your own loved ones' lives. These prophecies are mostly Bible verses that I read during my daily devotional Bible reading. I claimed them for my son because I knew the Word of God is alive and living, and when I released the Word of God by faith over him, I also knew the dead bones must respond—those bones can't help but come back to life!

For the word of God is alive and active. Sharper than any double-edged sword, it penetrates even to dividing soul and spirit, joints and marrow; it judges the thoughts and attitudes of the heart (Hebrews 4:12).

Remember, Jesus is our example, and He showed us in the Garden of Gethsemane that every battle is won in our mind first, before it is fought on the battlefield, so get a conquering mindset and fight on your children's behalf. Prophesy, mamas and daddies! Call down the four winds and say, "Come O breath of God. Breathe life back into my child that they may live." Call your child by name!

Now here's the most exciting part: when I actively participated in the war by declaring the Word of God over him (because the Word of God is alive and living), the once dead, and dry bones started responding to God's Word and came back to life!

- I declare my son has a special heritage (Psalm 112:2-7).
- I declare that my son is one of God's chosen holy people, and The LORD is his God.
- I declare that my son has a new heart, and Your Spirit dwells in him, sovereign Lord.
- I declare that he will be a man of holy, godly character, a son of God, a mighty warrior in God's army.
- I declare that my son is careful to follow all of your decrees and keeps your laws, which are written on his heart.
- I declare that he will be honored everywhere he goes as a man of God.
- I declare that when darkness tries to overtake him, light will come bursting in.
- I declare that he will not be overthrown by evil circumstances, but God's constant care of him will make a deep impression on all who see it.
- I declare that he will not fear bad news, nor live in dread of what may happen, for he is settled in his mind that Jehovah will take care of him.

- I declare that he will bring joy to the Lord and make Him laugh with delight.
- I declare that he is marked for the kingdom of God.
- I declare that he is the head and not the tail.
- I declare that he is blessed with a strong will to do what God has called him to do, and with self-control and self-discipline.
- I declare that he is blessed with God's supernatural wisdom, and he will have clear direction for his life.
- I declare that he will have an obedient heart and positive outlook on life.
- I declare that any curse that has ever been spoken over him or any negative or evil word that has ever come against him is broken right now in Jesus' name.
- I declare that each thing he puts his hands to do will to prosper and succeed.
- I declare that he will find a Proverbs 31 woman to marry, a woman of beauty and filled with God's character and grace.
- I declare that he will be delivered from the traps and strongholds of Satan and live a life in Christ that's free indeed.
- I declare that these dry, dead bones will live, according to Ezekiel 37!

One day, after having spoken these prophecies over my son's life in daily prayer, the Lord said to me, "You have a mandate from heaven. Your prayers and prophecies are being fulfilled."

I can't tell you how excited I was after hearing those encouraging words. Then I got even more excited after looking up what the word *mandate* meant.

mandate: An official or authoritative command; an order or injunction; a commission.[1]

My friend, I believe God has the same mandate for your loved one too, therefore I want to encourage you again—Prophesy, mamas! Prophesy, daddies! Prophesy to what is dead and dry in your child's life. Speak to it, call it by name, and tell it to hear the word of the Lord and come back to life! As you do this by faith, God is going to make His word speak loudly to your loved ones—a rattling noise they can't help but hear!

So I prophesied as I was commanded: and as I prophesied, there was a noise, and, behold, an earthquake; and the bones came together, bone to its bone (Ezekiel 37:7 ASV).

This is the same biblical principle Jesus was talking about when he said, *Therefore I tell you, whatever you ask for in prayer, believe that you have received it, and it will be yours* (Mark 11:24).

My son's circumstances were speaking loudly to him, and he was shaken by the thought of serving years in prison. The Lord will also shake your loved one's dead bones to get their full attention back on Him. He's going to show them what is required of them as a child of the living God, as well as what things have eternal value.

Although God loves us, He will not shield us from the righteous requirements of a son of God. With that being said, don't be discouraged because of where they are right now, whether in jail, prison, or living around bad influences. This could very well be God's time of waking them up on the inside—a good spiritual clean-up and check-up!

So believe and stand firm in your faith and you *will* receive whatsoever you ask for in prayer.

Rejoice always, pray without ceasing, give thanks in all circumstances; for this is the will of God in Christ Jesus for you. (1 Thessalonians 5:16-18 ESV).

Get a new vision in your mind of what your child will look like in his or her mighty armor, with the glory of God permeating from every fiber of their being. Believe you will see the glory of God rise up in your child.

6

A Warrior Rises Up

You will be my people, and I will be your God (Ezekiel 36:28)

When Jesus' friend Martha told Him not to go into her brother Lazarus's tomb because he'd been dead for four days, Jesus said to her, *"Did I not tell you that if you believe, you will see the glory of God?"* (John 11:40).

When he had said this, Jesus called in a loud voice, "Lazarus, come out!" (John 11:43).

And a dead man came to life!

How many years has your child been spiritually dead? How much death has been caused by the things your child has done? Has their life begun to decay and stink? Does all look hopeless? Then stand back, because if you have been prophesying as I encouraged you to do in the last chapter, then you have called forth the Word of the living God! That Word is about to enter your child like a lightning bolt—God is breathing life back into those dry, dead bones and saying, *come out of that grave!*

Notice that it says Jesus called in a loud voice. When prophesying over your loved ones, don't be afraid to get loud. Declare and decree the prophecy as if it's your battle cry!

The Word of God tells us that the walls of Jericho came down when the warriors of God gave a loud shout (Joshua 6:20). So *shout!* This is your great weapon of warfare against the powers of hell. The shouts of the saints are the atomic bomb God uses to bring down the powers of hell!

God has ascended amid shouts of joy, the Lord amid the sounding of trumpets. (Psalm 47:5).

For the Lord himself shall descend from heaven with a shout (1 Thessalonians 4:16 KJV).

When the trumpets sounded, the army shouted, and at the sound of the trumpet, when the men gave a loud shout, the wall collapsed; so everyone charged straight in, and they took the city. (Joshua 6:20).

It's time to charge straight into the battle zone and take your child back. You are in a war for your child's soul—and wars get loud! Great commanders make great commands, so rise up, warrior and fall into formation—God is calling forth His earthly army. The enemy of your soul has *declared war on you*—it's time to fight back!

Today you must make a choice: either you will lie down like a scared dog and become another witness to Satan's destruction, or you will begin to rise up and participate in the battle with the Lord of hosts and join in the fight!

Have I not commanded you? Be strong and courageous. Do not be terrified; do not be discouraged, for the LORD your God will be with you wherever you go (Joshua 1:9).

It's time to rise up and take back what the enemy has stolen from you!

***

Dive right into the training manual, God's Word, and get to know your enemy's cunning strategies and what you're up against. Because you'll need to have God's spiritual insight and His strategic battle plan if you're set on victory. Especially if you plan on defeating the enemy at every turn. The good news is, because of your direct line through Jesus Christ, you can go straight to the source. The truth is, if you're following the battle instructions God gave me, you're already completely engaged in the spiritual realm . . . fighting by faith, not by sight, as you wrestle against the rulers of this dark world.

For we wrestle not against flesh and blood, but against principalities, against powers, against the rulers of the darkness of this world, against spiritual wickedness in high places (Ephesians 6:12 KJV)

We see from this scripture that this battle goes beyond what we can see in the visible realm. God makes it obvious that this battle must be fought in the spirit realm, where by faith we trust that the warring angels of God are fighting with us against Satan and the powers of hell!

Elisha prayed, Open his eyes, LORD, so that he may see." Then the LORD opened the servant's eyes, and he looked and saw the hills full of horses and chariots of fire all around Elisha (2 Kings 6:17).

Do not fear the valley or the evil in it, because your victorious Lord and Savior Jesus Christ, the Commander of Heaven's Armies, goes before you with His mighty army and chariots of fire! Whom shall you fear?

So do not fear, for I am with you; do not be dismayed, for I am your God. I will strengthen you and help you; I will uphold you with my righteous right hand (Isaiah 41:10).

Although you may feel like you're fighting in the dark, reach out and take hold of the Lord's hand. He is the light that will pierce the darkness all around you and show you the way. He will fight fearlessly by your side until the war is over. Not only that, He will be faithful to instruct you in your role throughout each of the battles you fight, especially when it feels like the darkness is closing in to overtake you. I promise, if you will stay focused on Him, His light will continue to burst in and lead the way through the darkness.

When darkness overtakes him, light will come bursting in (Psalm 112:4 TLB).

The truth is, there are times we're better off not seeing, because if we could see all that we're up against, we may be too terrified to join in the fight. More importantly, if we could see the results of our faith right away, it wouldn't be faith at all.

The Word tells us what godly faith is:

Now faith is confidence in what we hope for and assurance about what we do not see (Hebrews 11:1).

God teaches us to be mighty warriors in the dark valley where we can't see a thing for a very good reason. He wants us to learn to follow His lead very closely, as we learn to trust Him. We do this as we keep advancing forward by faith through this weary, dark place. I'm reminded of the orders the officers gave the Israelites before crossing over the Jordan River, right before God took them into the Promised Land:

After three days the officers went throughout the camp, giving orders to the people: "When you see the ark of the covenant of the Lord your God, and the Levitical priests carrying it, you are to move out from your positions and follow it. Then you will know which way to go, since you have never been this way before" (Joshua 3:2-4).

If you want to get on into your Promised Land, then you have to follow God's orders closely. You may be standing at a new door today, and God is saying, *Follow me closely because I am about to take you through a wilderness you have never been through before.* If so, don't move out from your position until God moves first.

***

As God leads you through this valley into His Promised Land, it's extremely important that you realize you're going into a whole new territory. One where the enemy has already gone before you, setting up many barriers and traps. To navigate your way through safely will require complete obedience and dependence on God. Also, keep in mind that your loved one or prodigal child is walking through a dark place too. Remember, God's Word says, *we wrestle not against flesh and blood.* Thus, remember, our battle is not against them. So please don't blame them or make them feel ashamed for the destruction they may have caused. That's exactly what the enemy wants you to do. Let's face it, right now, they are standing at a new door too. Believe me, Satan's already heaping red-hot coals of condemnation on them. Oh yes, he's trying his best to steal their true identity and bring them into a hopeless and defeated state of mind.

Trust me, Satan's trying to use this time to set up some barriers between you and your loved one. This bait of offense or barrier must be taken out right away if you want both of you to enter the Promised Land together. Instead, encourage them with love and support during their dark hour, in the new man or woman that God is making them into. Tell them, "You were made for so much more!"

Get a new vision in your mind of them. Try to imagine them wearing their new glorified armor, placed there by God. See them smiling and shining bright with their new glorious light from God's presence on them. Try to imagine how wonderful it will be when you see God using their new light to pierce the darkness that once ruled over their lives? I can't tell you the impact it had on my son when we showed him nothing but unconditional love. Speak the truth, yes, but remember to always speak the truth in love.

Instead, speaking the truth in love (Ephesians 4:15).

Again, they are most likely already feeling defeated, frightened, and alone as they sit in their jail cells, whether it's a figurative cell or a literal one. The truth is, they are far away from God right now. Even sadness and depression can feel like a jail cell. So whatever form of captivity they are bound by, speak words of life, not death to them. Remember, *love never fails* (1 Corinthians 13:8).

Burst through that barrier. To get to the Promised Land, you have to take out everything that stands in your way. You may be very upset with your child for all the destruction they have caused. That's understandable. Trust me, I can relate! To be perfectly honest, I'll never forget how upset I would get with my son when we were trying to get him to realize how destructive his lifestyle was, but he just would not listen. At times I would think about the situation and become so angry with him. My mind would be plagued with the hurtful words he would say while we argued, not to mention the disrespect he showed us by doing exactly what we asked him not to do. To be honest, there were times that I found myself internalizing the pain and taking everything personally.

Trust me, the reality of our disobedience to God's instructions started to bear down upon my soul after we got him out of jail the first time. Everything seemed to accelerate from that moment on as the defiance grew stronger and more destructive. I know many of you can relate to these painful emotions. At that time, I felt like I had a right to be angry with him, and perhaps I did. There is such a thing as righteous indignation over mistreatment and injustice.

But one morning everything changed as the Lord awakened me and began to reason with me about my tormenting thoughts and righteous indignation. First, He reminded me of how much He loved me, then He reminded me of His forgiveness that was extended to me when I was in full blown rebellion as a young person. He took me back to the love I had for my children, when they were still young, pure, and innocent. He revealed to me something I had never realized before that day. He showed me the only person other than Himself who knows a child's true identity, *the real person* they are, is a parent or the person who raised them. What a deep revelation!

Think about it; we, as parents, are the only ones who saw the true, pure person God originally made our children to be, while they were still innocent children. We knew them better than anyone—even better than they knew themselves. During this precious time, we saw all the potential, strengths, and weaknesses within them, yet we loved them dearly just as they were, unconditionally . . . just as God loves us. What a wonderful privilege we were given to know the true, pure spirit of that little person God created.

God took me back that morning to who my son really was and how He wanted me to see him. From that moment on, my heart and the way I viewed my son was completely changed. I no longer blamed him for our painful circumstances or held his hurtful words against him. From the depths of my heart, I prayed and asked God to forgive me for holding on to the pain and destruction that went on during this time and then I forgave him too. You might say, I gave up my right to be angry with him. From that day forward, when I looked at my son, I remembered who he *really* was, long before the evil one stole him away from me.

I truly believe this is the way God sees all of His children. The person who is hidden from everyone else, even from themselves—the person He created them to be. God sees their true state and the pure spirit that He placed inside of them before the evil one defiled their soul with sin and took their spirit captive. In reality, that's *His* captive child, and His relentless love for them will never give up on them, nor will He leave or forsake them—and nor should we!

Beloved, now we are children of God, and what we will be has not yet been revealed. We know that when He appears, we will be like Him, for we will see Him as He is (1 John 3:2 BLB).

The writer is telling us who we are . . . His children. And who we really are has not yet been seen; but when He appears to us, we will be like Him. Let's face it: we don't even know who we really are, let alone who others are. Nevertheless, there's one thing I've seen over and over again: when Jesus makes Himself known in a person's heart and they begin to yield to His will and make Him their Lord and Savior, a transformation starts to take place. I saw this firsthand in my son's life. The amazing young man I once knew started to emerge again! God's glory and His likeness was radiant in him. I've seen this in so many of His precious saints. I'm sure you can say the same thing. I believe this is what the purification and sanctification process is all about. He is transforming us into His image as we yield to His will. Oftentimes this can be a very painful process.

And we all, who with unveiled faces contemplate the Lord's glory, are being transformed into his image with ever-increasing glory, which comes from the Lord, who is the Spirit. (2 Corinthians 3:18).

It's amazing how God's perspective changes everything, even our heart toward others as we see their true identity through His eyes.

The Lord does not look at the things people look at. People look at the outward appearance, but the Lord looks at the heart (1 Samuel 16:7).

Every time I was with my son after having this experience with the Lord, I appealed to his heart and imparted life and love through my words right into his spirit. I would use our valuable time together to tell him who he really was in God's eyes. Satan always wants us to identify with our past and see ourselves as defeated and undeserving of love. But God sees what He placed inside of us—the undefiled spirit man. That's who we *really* are. And one day, we will receive our everlasting glorified bodies to go along with our new glorified spirit man.

It's time to see what God sees and focus on what God says we are, not what the Devil wants us to see and believe about ourselves or others. This is why Satan is called the accuser of the brethren, and why he constantly reminds all of us of our past failures.

For the accuser of our brothers and sisters, who accuses them before our God day and night, has been hurled down (Revelation 12:10).

If Satan can get us to believe his lies, then we will never see ourselves or others for who they really are. This is why we need to recognize his evil strategies, or *traps*. If we don't, how will we ever rise up to be the person God intended us to be, let alone encourage others to reach the true purpose God has for them.

There's nothing more powerful than seeing a person begin to believe who they really are in Christ and then watching them rise up and take hold of their God-given identity!

Please understand, I'm not telling you to let your loved one walk all over you. I just want to encourage you to stand firm in your love for that person, even if it means using the tough love of their circumstances to reach them. You never know; the Lord may require you to use some tough love for a time. That doesn't mean you don't show them unconditional love while they're in the midst of their circumstances. Sometimes, they need to get a good look at the reality of what they've done to themselves and others. Don't be afraid to let the circumstances of their surroundings speak loudly, if that is what God is requiring of you at this time. This is another reason why it's so important to take your cues and instructions from God. He knows where your child is spiritually and what they may need at that time.

Only in the valley can God get you to a place of complete dependence on your Deliverer! Only in deep darkness can you learn to walk by faith and not by sight. Everything that is of you will be driven out of you by the time you finally step out of this valley floor. Trust me, you will never be the same again. Just like the three disciples Jesus took to the top of the mountain were never the same again after He revealed to them His glory. By faith, I will make you the same promise Jesus made Martha—if you will *believe* and stay in the fight, you too will see His glory show up again and again as you walk through the valley below.

David said about him: "'I saw the Lord always before me. Because he is at my right hand, I will not be shaken'" (Acts 2:25).

The Lord is my light and my salvation—whom shall I fear? The Lord is the stronghold of my life—of whom shall I be afraid? (Psalm 27:1).

With those insightful words from King David in mind, I will ask you again: *Can these dry bones live?* To which God says, *Yes, they can!*

So keep on prophesying and calling back not only your dreams for your child, but God's dreams. Pray without ceasing and call back God's original divine purpose and destiny for them . . . call these things that are not yet in existence as though they already were. You can trust *the God who gives life to the dead and calls into being things that were not* (Romans 4:17).

Stand on the promises of God as you believe by faith that the Lord will bring all these things to pass.

God is not human, that he should lie, not a human being, that he should change his mind. Does he speak and then not act? Does he promise and not fulfill? (Numbers 23:19).

***

As I close out another chapter, I want to leave you with this thought:

just as it takes time to form a human being in a mother's womb, it will take time to train up a mighty warrior of God, one filled with God's holy character and true spiritual grit. During this time of disciplining, God is asking you to trust Him and believe He will protect your child and do in their life what He promised to do in the life of His beloved Israelite children . . . raise up another warrior for His glorious earthly army. He asked the same of me, and I can tell you now, it was worth all the pain and suffering we went through. Why? Because it was during that difficult and trying time that I witnessed a complete miracle taking place. As I watched in amazement, God brought my son's dead, dry bones back to life again! Not only did I watch Him bring my son back to life, I was able to see how He used his time of captivity as a good training ground. As it turned out, the valley was the perfect ground for training up God's mighty warrior. Yes, my son was being trained in God's boot camp of captivity, just like the Israelites, to be one of His mighty warriors!

Like Ezekiel, as I prophesied, things started to come together for my son. He was beginning to talk and act like a responsible and righteous man of God. But God wasn't finished yet, and neither was I. There was still much work to do, so I kept prophesying to those dry bones by faith and believed that the breath of God would continue to breathe on him and enter into those areas of his life that still needed to be made whole. I was *confident* God would raise him from that valley of death completely whole.

Then he said to him, "Rise and go; your faith has made you well" (Luke 17:19).

Yes, I *believed* he would rise up out of that valley and be the mighty warrior God purposed him to be and become a vital part of God's holy earthly army. Interestingly enough, my son wasn't the only one who was being trained and transformed during that time. My husband and I were being trained too. So don't be surprised, my friend, when you see a transformation taking place in your own spiritual life during this time of training. This will be a time of glorious transformation all right, as He takes you and your loved one from glory to *every-increasing glory.*

7

Hearing God When He Speaks

My sheep hear my voice; and I know them,
and they follow me (John 10:27 KJV).

Jesus is always speaking, but we never know how His voice will come to us. The truth is, our Lord wants to communicate with His people, and He wants the freedom to speak however He chooses. It may be through dreams, visions, books, billboards, the Bible, or even through a true prophet of the Lord. Without a doubt, His voice can often take on several different forms. But when you hear His voice—you know it.

I'm reminded of when the prophet Elijah desperately needed to hear God's voice. At this time, he was running for his life and hiding in a cave. As he sought the Lord for help, he was instructed by God to: *"Go out and stand on the mountain in the presence of the Lord, for the Lord is about to pass by." Then a great and powerful wind tore the mountains apart and shattered the rocks before the Lord, but the Lord was not in the wind. After the wind there was an earthquake, but the Lord was not in the earthquake. After the earthquake came a fire, but the Lord was not in the fire. And after the fire came a gentle whisper* (1 Kings 19:11-12). The Bible tells us when Elijah heard it, he knew it was the voice of the Lord.

Sometimes God speaks to us in order to exhort and encourage us to do something that is part of His purpose and plan for our lives. Other times God will speak in various ways to correct us or warn us of impending danger for ourselves or others. This has happened to me several times through dreams. My personal favorite is when He gives me an inspiration or revelation about something I need to do, then I know exactly what to do at that very moment. Other times, I will have a strange feeling about something, and seek His counsel. But for the most part, I hear His *still, small voice (or whisper.)* Whatever means God chooses to speak, we need to heed His voice and follow His leading.

God said, *This is my Son, whom I love. Listen to him!* (Mark 9:7). The Father spoke those words while Peter, James, and John were with Jesus, when He was transfigured before their eyes. God spoke to them in an audible voice and the message was clear: *Listen to him!*

I can honestly say, I have never heard God's audible voice. However, my husband did hear the audible voice of God one morning in church during the worship service. The Lord spoke two words to him that day: *Stop drinking!* Although neither of us thought he had a drinking problem at that time, in obedience to the Lord, my husband heeded His voice and stopped drinking. Also, at this time, our oldest son was only three years old, and we had no idea that he would someday struggle with alcoholism. But God knew, and He didn't give an explanation of why He was making this request, but, looking back now, we see clearly how He used my husband's obedience to work all things together for our good. I can't begin to imagine the guilt my husband would have experienced if he didn't heed God's voice of warning and later realized he had inadvertently influenced our son's alcoholism.

At this time, I had already followed the Lord's leading to stop drinking. I was a social drinker and, for the most part, I could take it or leave it. To be honest, the reason I thought God was leading me to stop drinking was to be more effective in sharing the gospel, because I knew drinking could pose a problem for those weaker in the faith who might be struggling with alcohol abuse. Now, with all that being said, please follow your own convictions about drinking alcohol, because I'm certainly not against social drinking or having a glass of wine, for that matter. I'm only sharing my story to encourage you to be obedient to the

Lord's leading.

As I said before, God is always speaking to us. We just need to pay attention and stop ignoring Him when He asks us to do something we really don't want to do or don't understand why He's asking it of us at the time.

Listen to my instruction and be wise; do not disregard it (Proverbs 8:33).

For example, the day my husband and I were asked to leave our son in jail for three days and three nights. That was the last thing I expected to hear that morning when His still, small voice spoke to me, and I certainly didn't understand at the time why God was asking something so difficult. Perhaps His voice was so gentle that it made ignoring it easier . . . big mistake! Once again, however His voice comes, we need to *obey it*. If He's speaking, it's important to not only hear His voice, but to obey it too.

But be doers of the word, and not hearers only, deceiving yourselves (James 1:22 ESV).

Jesus often chose to speak in parables, which took some interpretation, but other times He spoke very clearly, leaving no room for misinterpretation. Oftentimes I will hear Him speaking to me through a written form, and when I do, it feels as if the words just jump off the page right at me. Trust me, when that happens, I don't need any interpretation. It's as though I can hear Him speaking those exact words to me. Other times, a story, phrase in a book, a personal conviction, or something prophesied over me will bring me to tears, and I know it's the Holy Spirit moving within my spirit, confirming His voice. I've had this to happen many times while in church, and you probably have too.

The truth is, we don't always know how He will speak, but I do know that being aware of the many different ways He does speak is very important. John Paul Jackson wrote a book called *The Art of Hearing God,* and I must say, it is an art that must be mastered if we want to know His ways and follow Him closely.

Now then, my children, listen to me; blessed are those who keep my ways (Proverbs 8:32).

I'll never forget how God used the written method to speak to me one night, and it didn't come through His Holy Bible, as it so often would. No, this time His voice came while I was reading an encouraging Christian book. We all know God's timing is always perfect. On this night His words couldn't have come at a better time. I later realized He was trying to teach me the importance and power of being decisive early on in my journey through the dark valley.

In the evenings following my son's arrest, I would read while I soaked in my tub as a way to relax or escape for a while. During that time especially, my reading choices were always spiritually uplifting and encouraging books. Because this was one of my darkest hours, I knew I needed all the encouragement I could get. The book I read this particular night was titled *An Enemy Called Average* by John L. Mason. Remember when I told you that I am just an average ordinary person? Well, this book will encourage you to not think that way if you want to do the extraordinary things God has intended for you to do! Obviously God thought I needed to change the way I thought about myself if I was going to become the courageous warrior He wanted me to be.

I found *An Enemy Called Average* to be a wonderful source of inspiration. As I continued the enjoyable nightly routine of reading what the author calls "nuggets," I turned the page to read the next short little nugget and, as I did, the words in the title seemed to jump off the page and resonate with my spirit. What that nugget taught was just what I needed to hear at that very moment. In essence, what it said was that I needed to make a decision, right then, that day, that I was going to get on through what I was going through.

At this time, I was halfway through the book, and, although I'd enjoyed each of the previous nuggets, none of them had hit me like this one did. I knew the Lord had just spoken to me directly out of my storm, much like He did with Job! Amazingly, it was the night before my son's sentencing. Only God knew that phrase in the title would be the nugget I would read that night. And there it was, just what I needed to hear, like a word spoken to me at God's perfect time. Oh yes, He was saying, *Daughter, it's time you make up your mind and get on through what you've been going through!*

The message God had for me was very clear. It was a nugget all right—one of solid gold! The Lord knew if I was going to live in the victory as instructed, I needed to settle the matter in my mind first. Why? Because that's where the battle is fought—in our minds! (Joyce Meyer wrote a powerful book about this never-ending battle, and I highly recommend you read it: *Battlefield of the Mind.*)

After receiving that powerful, solid word from the Lord, I knew it was time to put it into action and make up my mind. Admittedly, I was already guilty of allowing the enemy to wear my mind out with fearful thoughts as I tried over and over again to figure everything out. As you know by now, the enemy doesn't need any help, but he is always happy to help out, especially if he can torment us and steal our joy and peace! Knowing this was the Lord speaking to me through those insightful words, I decided that night to set my mind on the victory and keep it set.

Set you minds on things above, not on earthly things (Colossians 3:2).

By that, I mean it was time for me to completely trust the God above, get on through what I had been going through, and stop trying to figure it all out . . . and that's exactly what I did! I made a deliberate choice to set my mind that night, and I knew in my heart that no matter what verdict the earthly judge read the next day, I was going to accept it as God's verdict and His perfect will for my son's life. I was determined to trust God as the only true and just Judge. Therefore I gave the verdict, the sentencing, and all that was on my mind over to the Lord that night in complete surrender.

The next morning, I walked into that courtroom with Jesus and my husband by my side. Although this was my first time to enter a courtroom, let alone waiting for my son's sentencing, I had God's perfect peace resting on me. I felt settled and completely confident that my God was in control. And wouldn't you just know it, He came through once again! Although things didn't go the way I thought they would go, I must say, it went much better than it could have.

At that time, I was on the 40th day of a fast for my son's sentencing, eating only one meal a day, and, needless to say, I was hungry! Having spent that time in fasting and prayer, I knew God's verdict had been given and I had finished my active part in this particular battle. So, with that, we left the courtroom and celebrated the Lord's verdict by eating my first breakfast in forty days. Yes, God's verdict was spoken that day and I was going to trust that He knew exactly what He was doing and why.

Remember how David fasted and prayed for the life of his baby son, but when the verdict was read and the baby was taken from him, he got up and ate:

He answered, "While the child was still alive, I fasted and wept. I thought, 'Who knows? The Lord may be gracious to me and let the child live'" (2 Samuel 12:22).

Here we see that David actively and patiently did his part in the battle, but, in the end, he submitted to the will of God. But God in His great mercy made it up to David by giving him Solomon—the wisest king that ever lived.

Things won't always turn out the way we hope, but that's where faith and trust come in and give us His amazing peace. As God used the words of John L. Mason to help me to make up my mind that night, I want to encourage you to make that same decision to get on with your life and to fulfill your divine purpose, despite your current circumstances. God wants each of us to come through whatever situations we face. We are not to be moved by what we see, but by the unseen hand of God.

Humble yourselves, therefore, under God's mighty hand, that he may lift you up in due time (1 Peter 5:6).

For we live by faith, not by sight (2 Corinthians 5:7).

We need to say to ourselves enough is enough! I'm sick and tired of going through this. I'm going to get on with my life and get on through it!

Oftentimes your circumstance won't change right away, and you may still have to go through the struggle of dealing with what may be in store for your loved one in prison or whatever dark place he or she finds themselves. But, either way, you must at some point decide to accept what you cannot change and make up your mind to change you. The sooner you come to this place in your journey, the better!

In difficult times such as this, the Serenity Prayer is the perfect prayer to pray. *Serenity* means the state of being calm, peaceful, and untroubled. The Serenity Prayer is a powerful and courageous prayer if you pray it with all your heart. As I walked through the darkest days of my life, God gave me the courage to accept the things I could not change and the wisdom to trust Him.

Trust me, I had no idea how to handle something like this; I was living in a whole new world—a world I never dreamed I would live in. I had no previous experience in this arena of hell, and I had no idea of how to face it either. Often times I felt as if I was walking in deep, gross darkness. Nevertheless, I did know I could trust the One who was holding my hand, and I knew if I didn't let go, He would lead me through that darkness. Not only that, I had a wonderful Teacher who was ready to teach and counsel me in all things, and He was living right inside of me.

But the counselor, the Holy Spirit whom the Father will send in my name, will teach you all things and remind you of everything I have told you (John 14:26 CSB).

Day by day, as I walked through the deep darkness of the valley below, I was counseled by the Holy Spirit and taught through God's living Word on how to remain stable, peaceful, and courageous. The definition for courage is: *that quality of mind which enables one to encounter danger and difficulties with firmness, or without fear, or fainting of heart.* Courage is the strength God gives us to confront our fears in the face of pain or grief. I call that God's supernatural strength! A strength that comes from being close to God.

"For who is he who will devote himself to be close to me?" declares the Lord (Jeremiah 30:21).

Stay as close to Him as you possibly can and learn His ways so you won't get lost while in the darkness. You will hear me say this over and over again throughout this book. Because there is nothing more important than walking in a close personal relationship with the Lord your God. The closer you are to someone, the easier it is to hear them when they speak. Also, to see when they are pointing out something that you need to see. It's the same with our proximity to God: . . . *find rest in the shadow of the Almighty* (Psalm 91:1 NLT). So, my friend, once again I want to encourage you to be open to hearing God's voice in whatever form God chooses to speak.

Praise God, I was able to break free of the enemy's evil trap as I heeded His voice. Yes, He exposed the trap I was caught in and released me from it on that faithful night. After that, He kept me moving forward so I wouldn't get stuck in Satan's intended trap of despair and defeat again. You see, Satan wants to keep our hour of darkness perpetual; it's like living on a dead-end street. Again, I'm so thankful that I heard God's voice that night and heeded the warning, I didn't let Satan keep me trapped on that dead-end street, wandering through the same old valley of regret and despair over and over again—and you shouldn't either.

Trust me when I say, I haven't forgotten what it felt like to wake up every morning in a spiritual jail and prison cell. Oh yes, that was a place of captivity that the enemy would have been thrilled to keep me in. But praise be to God, I broke free of those prison bars, and you can too, by not entertaining his fearful debilitating thoughts any longer.

I learned how to escape that prison cell by placing all of my fears and worries completely in God's faithful hands. I'm not saying I never struggled with fear and anxiety from that point on. Oh no, that didn't happen all at once, at least not for me. But with God's help, I eventually learned to daily make that important decision not to listen to the lies of the enemy. I was determined to not lean to my own understanding, but to walk out my faith, trusting my son's life to my Almighty, faithful God. With His perfect peace as my guide and sign, I knew God was working everything together for our good. This is His promise to all believers.

And we know that in all things God works for the good of those who love him, who have been called according to his purpose for them (Romans 8:28 NLT).

You will keep in perfect peace those whose minds are steadfast, because they trust in you (Isaiah 26:3).

As I said before, I did my part in raising my son for God. Therefore it came as no surprise to me when one day the Lord said to me, *Daughter, you have done what I told you to do. Now let go and let me do what I'm going to do.* That day, I knew it was time for letting go!

Maybe you too have been holding on to your loved one and can't stop worrying and fretting over them either. Please trust God and let them go out of your arms into His. Give them one last hug and say to the Lord, "Out of my arms into Yours, Jesus!" If you can't give your child a hug physically, then visualize this in your mind and give them one last big hug in the spirit, and then release them into the Lord's loving arms. I can't put into words how freeing that was. From that day on, every time I hugged my son goodbye and let go of him, I would say those words to the Lord: *Out of my arms into yours, O Lord.* This simple yet powerful act of faith made all of the difference in the world for me. It helped me to move on and get on through what I was going through. If you don't start taking deliberate steps in a forward motion, you will keep living the same old defeated life—alive but not living. You will be a captive in Satan's vicious and never-ending trap of despair. It's time to stop that vicious cycle of defeat and move out from that prison cell, my friend!

Charlotte Jewell

Arise, let us go from here.(John 14:31 NKJV)

8

Being Mighty through God

For though we live in the world, we do not wage war as the world does.
The weapons we fight with are not the weapons of the world. On the
contrary, they have divine power to demolish strongholds.
We demolish arguments and every pretension that sets itself up against
the knowledge of God (2 Corinthians 10:3-5).

Unfortunately, God is not the only one who speaks to us. Satan is very
cunning and, according to the Word of God, can appear as an angel of
light.

For Satan himself masquerades as an angel of light (2 Corinthians
11:14).

Satan owns the art of deceiving people, and he loves to speak his lies into
the ears of God's people too. He says things like, *God has failed you! or*
You're a good person, so why has God let all these bad things happen to
you? He wasn't there for you when you needed Him the most. If you start
believing these lies, not only will he continue to destroy everything you
hold dear in this world, he will soon lead you into the dark trap of
despair. Before long, you will find yourself mad at God and blaming
Him. This is one of Satan's most deadly and deceptive traps! This is
what Paul was talking about when he wrote 2 Corinthians 10:3-5. The
King James Version of verse 4 in this passage says it this way: *For the*
weapons of warfare are not carnal, but mighty through God to the
pulling down of strong holds. From reading this scripture, we know that

the only way we can pull down this lie (stronghold) of the evil one is to use God's divine weapons of warfare that are mighty *through Him.*

But what if Satan has deceived us and caused us to be mad at God? Can we still pull down these strongholds of the evil one without God's help? I would say no, because, without God's help, we have no power to defeat the enemy of our soul. Oh yes, we have His divine weapons as born again believers, but they are powerless if He's not allowed access to our hearts to activate them. You might say we have the gun, but He has the fire power! Sincere and willful repentance is the only way to open the floodgates of our closed off heart toward God and let His power once again flow *through* us.

That's why the enemy is always trying to plant seeds of bitterness and unforgiveness in our hearts toward God and others. He knows if he can fill our hearts with this powerful, deadly stronghold, we will be powerless to stop him! When we choose to hold on to a grudge and nurse it in our hearts, we are allowing seeds of bitterness to pollute our souls, therefore clogging up our spiritual lifeline that goes straight to God. If these seeds are left in place, they have the potential to contaminate our entire being like a fast-growing cancer. Only through true repentance and forgiveness of this deadly sin can those seeds be completely eradicated and pulled out by the roots.

But if you do not forgive others their sins, your Father will not forgive your sins (Matthew 6:15). Again, this is Jesus speaking to born again believers. This is not just another good idea, or something out of the Old Testament. This is a commandment that comes with a grave consequence if not heeded.

The Word of God tells us that God flows through clean, pure vessels. *Those who cleanse themselves from the latter will be instruments for special purposes, made holy, useful to the Master and prepared to do any good work* (2 Timothy 2:21). This cleansing from God comes through forgiveness; it is His way of making us pure and holy so we can be used for His *special purposes.* When we are living in this pure state of holiness, we can easily recognize and destroy any evil work of darkness that may try to attach itself to us. There's no power that can stand against us when God is flowing through us using His divine weapons! Never forget that Satan and his warriors of this dark world know this all too well. And that my friend is why he speaks his lies into the minds of God's *people*. He knows how powerful it is if he can convince you of this lie, and, trust me, nothing causes God's precious people to get dangerously stuck in the valley more often than this deadly trick of the enemy. In fact, this trap is so serious, it's like a graveyard to the Christians' hopes, dreams, and destinies! Not only for them, but also for their loved ones who need to break free from these strongholds of the evil one too.

I strongly urge you to avoid this deadly trap by asking God to forgive you for holding unforgiveness in your heart toward Him or anyone else. Don't get stuck in the valley because you are mad at God! Again, if you take this mindset of anger toward God, Satan can utterly destroy everyone and everything you hold precious in this world.

Satan is always trying to twist hurting people's minds during their weakened state. He knows just when to strike, and just what to say . . . he is always crouching around the corner, just waiting for that perfect moment. If he can get you to turn on God and see Him as the enemy, then he has already won the war. The rest will be easy for him, and he knows it! Why? Because you aren't engaged in the battle, let alone rightly joined with God to fight through you. Again, I'm not saying God's going to give up on you. No, His Word says He will never leave us or forsake us. But it's as though we have given up on Him. How this must grieve His heart! Please believe me when I say, Satan won't just stop there—he will go after everything you hold dear as he holds you in a place of rebellion against God. Not only that, if you are fighting with God and questioning His Holy character, according to the Word, you could be in serious danger:

Woe to those who quarrel with their Maker (Isaiah 45:9).

Again, getting God's people stuck in bitterness and anger toward

Him (or others) is one of Satan's most powerful strongholds! If you don't watch out for this trap, he will tie you up and hold you captive for the rest of your life. You will never be able to get out of the wilderness valley. He will hold you in a prison cell of despair, self-pity and defeat until God sends someone or He comes Himself and breaks Satan's grip on you by boldly speaking the truth in love. Trust me, Satan will give you every good and justified reason to be mad at God, or anyone else, just to assure his victory over you! Don't forget, what the heart believes, the mind justifies.

I'm not trying to be judgmental, but oftentimes, when I heard someone tell me how mad they were at God when tragedy struck, I couldn't help but notice they were also lacking in their personal relationship with Him. Let's face it: if you truly know someone in a close, personal way, their character is never in question—you know that you can trust them. When tragedy struck my family, the last thing that came to my mind was to be mad at God! I knew who my enemy was, and it certainly wasn't the sweet, loving Lord and Savior I had come to know. Yes, God allows certain things to happen in our lives that we would prefer didn't take place. He certainly has the power to stop the enemy, that's for sure. But His Holy character tells me there's a very good reason why He isn't intervening right now.

Think about it: if you don't really know Him well enough to trust Him with the most difficult trials of your life, how can you trust Him to take you into heaven when that time comes? You see, it's a vicious circle that the enemy wants to keep you going around and around in, and it's straight out of the pit of hell. If the Devil can keep you mad at God, then you won't draw near to Him for the help you need, and the Devil knows that too. God's the only one who can break the powers of darkness that roam to and fro across the earth, seeking whom they may devour. Again, Satan knows this, and that's why he uses this stronghold over and over again on Christian believers who have shallow relationships with God. They are easy prey! The truth is, we need to make up our minds: either God is who He says He is or He's not . . . we can't be double minded when things aren't going our way.

But when you ask, you must believe and not doubt, because the one who doubts is like a wave of the sea, blown and tossed by the wind. That person should not expect to receive anything from the Lord (James 1:6-7).

Are you struggling with unforgiveness because someone is raging against you right now, and somehow you feel justified to hold on to your unforgiveness? The Lord promises us that *all who rage against you will surely be ashamed and disgraced; those who oppose you will be as nothing and perish* (Isaiah 41:11). With that being said, let God handle the enemy and all those who are raging against you right now, and get on with what He has called you to do. Don't let seeds of bitterness trap you in this evil valley when the Promised Land is just up ahead.

I must be honest, this concept of being mad at God wasn't something I had given much thought to when I began writing this book. Maybe it was because I didn't get mad at God when the evil one came knocking at my door. It just wasn't something the enemy tried to challenge me on. However, when I was getting close to the end of writing this book, I began to tell some people what I was writing about and my difficult trials throughout my journey. This often led to them telling me about their trials as well. I must say, I was shocked as I noticed that many of them were furiously mad at God because they didn't understand why He was allowing these bad things to happen in their lives. Have we as Christians forgotten that we live in a fallen world, where the Devil and his evil ones prowl around looking for someone to devour?

Be alert and of sober mind. Your enemy the devil prowls around like a roaring lion looking for someone to devour (1 Peter 5:8).

Some justified their anger by saying things like, "God understands our anger." Well, I know Him pretty well by now, and I believe that may be true, because God is very patient with us, but I can't help but think how it must grieve His heart terribly to see His children mad at Him for something He didn't do.

Have you ever had someone you love with all your heart mad at you for something you didn't do, but even with all your best efforts, you couldn't convince them otherwise? I know someone I love dearly who lives a life of shame for something she never did, all because the Devil used someone to build up a stronghold (lie) against her. As always, it started with deception. You see, the Devil deceived a trusted member of our family, convincing her to believe a lie, and he was able to do so because the circumstances that surrounded this situation made it look like the truth. Although that was sad and destructive enough, it didn't stop there. The family member who had been deceived then took the lie and spoke it as if it was the truth to the woman's children! Unfortunately, the children were deceived by this awful lie too, and, because the lie came from someone they trusted, in their minds, it was the gospel truth! Needless to say, a trail of destruction and tears continues to follow this poor mother, even to this day.

This is a perfect example of a very serious stronghold. Circumstances may scream, *it's the truth!* But be not deceived!

But I am afraid that just as Eve was deceived by the serpent's cunning, your minds may somehow be led astray from your sincere and pure devotion to Christ (2 Corinthians 11:3).

The truth is, once a stronghold has been reinforced by someone who is trusted, it's almost impossible to pull down. Only by the power of God and an open heart of the one holding on to this stronghold can the truth pull it down! Again, more destruction and division brought on by the greatest liar and deceiver of all times—Satan! He has this thing mastered!

And why wouldn't he? He's been doing it for thousands of years, ever since he first deceived a third of God's angels, convincing them to follow him in rebellion against God. And don't forget about Adam and Eve, who passed this rebellious sin nature on down to us.

Jesus said this about Satan: *When he lies, he speaks his native language, for he is a liar and the father of lies* (John 8:44). The devastation caused by this father of lies and his evil deception has destroyed countless lives.

Perhaps you or your loved one has been falsely accused of a crime they never committed. If so, you know the injustice and overwhelming anger that goes along with that pain. I too know the crushing pain of that injustice, because my son went to prison and had his reputation destroyed by false accusations made against him. Oh yes, the circumstances screamed, "He's guilty!" But God knew the truth, and everything the old Devil meant for evil, God has turned around and used for our good ever since.

My friend, no matter how badly you feel about being betrayed, don't hold on to the offense. Forgive the offender from the depths of your heart and trust God to right the wrong done to you. The truth is, if God is allowing it for now, let Him have His way. He alone knows why He's allowing it and what He plans on doing to make it up to you. Take it from someone who knows. He has a very good reason, or He would not have allowed it at all.

I struggled with this stronghold myself for a long time, but with God's help and because I eventually came to a place of complete surrender to God's will, I was able to let it go and forgive the entire justice system. To God be all the glory for helping me pull down that powerful stronghold!

But that wasn't the only time I had to reach a place of complete surrender to God's will. Not long after I surrendered that stronghold to the Lord, I was challenged with another Satanic stronghold—one he built up against me for years. Sadly, it was with someone I dearly loved and treasured as a person.

When it first happened, I felt like I was being punished for something I didn't do—because I was! And believe me, it was heartbreaking. Even so, until a person is ready to hear your side of the story and give you a chance to plead your case, that stronghold will remain firmly in place.

As my heart broke over the stronghold Satan built up with my loved one, I began to pray for God's wise counsel on how to pull it down. God was faithful to give me the perfect battle plan—unconditional love! In other words, God told me to show her nothing except unconditional love, no matter what she did or said to me. As soon as He gave me this battle strategy, I knew it was a full-proof plan. Why? Because the Word of God tells us, *love never fails* (1 Corinthians 13:8).

I quickly activated this perfect plan, but things didn't change overnight. There were many difficult tests along the way. But slowly yet surely, I started to see the strongholds lifting. When they did, I began to pray and fast for God to open the door for me to plead my case. Praise God, when that door was finally opened, it opened wide! And the only one who was allowed to enter through that door was me and God—Satan was not permitted!

God's grace was poured out that night like a mighty rushing river as He worked mightily through me to pull down every one of those strongholds! It was incredible how powerfully He spoke through me as she brought up one objective after the other. I stood my ground and spoke the truth in love. By the time that trial was over, Satan's strongholds (lies) lay defeated on the ground! This treasured relationship was completely restored, and I was finally exonerated from all wrongdoing!

The Word of God says, *Then you will know the truth, and the truth will set you free* (John 8:32). Jesus wants to set us free from anything that would bind us up, especially the Devil's strongholds. Those strongholds are the lies he uses to build a case against us and turn the hearts of those we love dearly against us. He will reinforce those lies and make them sound and look as though they are the gospel truth for as long as we allow him. Keep in mind, what the heart believes, the mind justifies. Again, this is the same old trick he uses when he tries to convince you that God is your enemy. As you may already know, it's a horrible feeling to know that you haven't done anything wrong, but someone who has believed the Devil's lie has now developed such a low opinion of you, that they somehow feel justified in treating you with disrespect. It's a deep, crushing pain that goes into the very core of your soul.

There is so much more I could say about the many different strongholds the enemy uses. These are just a few examples. I encourage you to study more on this important topic to understand how strongholds may be affecting your spiritual walk, even now. Learn how strongholds attach themselves to your soul, and how destructive they can be to Christians and unbelievers too.

My friend, I knew I had to add this chapter somewhere near the beginning of the battle instructions God has given me to share with you. And this is why: I can share my story with you and try to encourage and build up your faith, but if you have unforgiveness in your heart against anyone, even yourself, it can keep you from being the useful vessel God wants and needs you to be right now. If you can go to that person and confess this sin of unforgiveness, please do so. Then ask them to forgive you. If it isn't possible to go to them, then take it to the Lord and confess it to Him, and ask for His forgiveness. After that, lay it down on His mercy seat and leave it there; don't burden yourself with it again, because God's Word says, He has cast it *as far as the east is from the west, so far has he removed our transgressions from us* (Psalm 103:12). When you do this, God will be faithful to forgive you and cleanse your heart once again . . . then look out, Devil!

Therefore, if you are offering your gift at the altar and there remember that your brother or sister has something against you, leave your gift there in front of the altar. First go and be reconciled to them; then come and offer your gift (Matthew 5:23-24).

Therefore confess your sins to each other and pray for each other so that you may be healed. The prayer of a righteous person is powerful and effective (James 5:16).

Once again, this is God's way of letting us know how important it is to forgive others. Perhaps we may even give them a chance to plead their case and ask forgiveness, thus bringing down the strongholds in their life too. May we all be freed from this trap of despair!

My friend, please know, until this stronghold has been pulled down, you may never walk in the victory that Christ died for you to have.

Not that I have already obtained all this, or have already arrived at my goal, but I press on to take hold of that for which Christ Jesus took hold of me (Philippians 3:12).

I the Lord search the heart and examine the mind, to reward each person according to their conduct, according to what their deeds deserve (Jeremiah 17:10).

So press on toward the mark and let it go so you can take hold of that for which Christ took hold of you!

My heart still breaks for my dear loved one who still suffers in silent pain because of the injustice that was done to her through a vicious lie that created a powerful stronghold. I can only hope someday soon her children will give her the benefit of the doubt, as my loved one did, and give her the same chance to set the record straight—once and for all. Again, it's up to the individual to open their hearts and forgive, but, until that time, they are a willing victim of the lie that became their sad reality—a stronghold of Satan!

How sad to think about how many people's lives have been ruined, and even their God-given destinies destroyed, because they believed a lie about someone else or even themselves. I once heard Joyce Meyer talk about this years ago in one of her insightful teachings on strongholds. In essence, she said that although it was never the truth, and will always be a lie, to the one who believes the lie, it has become their reality. Unfortunately, many people have fallen victim to this vicious deception. Again, this is just another example of "what the heart believes the mind justifies." Our heart, biblically speaking, is composed of our mind, our will, our emotion, and our conscience. In essence, our heart thinks, decides, and senses right from wrong. The Word of God tells us that: *The heart is deceitful above all things, and desperately wicked: who can know it?* (Jeremiah 17:9 KJV). Therefore, strongholds can only be pulled down by knowing the truth and the mighty power of God! *Then you will know the truth, and the truth will set you free* (John 8:32).

The Bible says: *The thief comes only to steal and kill and destroy; I have come that they may have life, and have it to the full* (John 10:10). And who is the thief that this scripture verse is referring to? The Devil! He's the real thief and father of all lies. Again, remember, a thief won't stop robbing you until he takes everything you have that has any value whatsoever! With that being said, please stop being mad at others, especially at God. Stop fighting the very one who wants to help you turn the Devil's weapons back on him.

It is for freedom that Christ has set us free. Stand firm, then, and do not let yourselves be burdened again by a yoke of slavery (Galatians 5:1)

.

9

Dwell in the Secret Place

How lovely is your dwelling place, LORD Almighty! (Psalm 84:1).

He who dwells in the secret place of the Most High shall abide under the shadow of the Almighty (Psalm 91:1-2 NKJV).

To live in the victory, you must keep your mind abiding *under the shadow of the Almighty* and remain steadfast in this place of safety and refuge until the battle is over. The Psalmist David called it "the secret place of the Most High." From reading these scripture verses, we see clearly where God wants us to dwell—near Him. He wants to be our dwelling place.

Moses said, *Lord, you have been our dwelling place throughout all generations* (Psalm 90:1). This is God's way of saying, dwell in my presence, abide in Me, and don't move out of this position until I move with you. In a way, you could say this is a prerequisite if you are bent on winning throughout the war. *For in him we live and move and have our being* (Acts 17:28). Every move we make must be done according to the leading of the Holy Spirit of God, whether it's a physical move or a mental move.

Psalms 91 goes on to say: *For he rescues you from every trap and protects you from the fatal plague. He will shield you with his wings! They will shelter you. His faithful promises are your armor. Now you don't need to be afraid of the dark anymore, nor fear the dangers of the day; nor dread the plagues of darkness, nor disasters in the morning* (Psalm 91:3-6 TLB).

God's protective wings are always open to His children. They are our shelter and refuge from the plagues of darkness and disaster. If you will remain close to Him and keep your mind stayed on Him, there is nothing to fear!

In one of her books, Joyce Meyers teaches that wherever we allow our mind to go, the rest of our selves will follow. Oh, how true that is! So be mindful of where you let your mind go or dwell. If left unchecked, the enemy will jump right in and take you where you don't need or want to go. He has a secret place too—an evil place, filled with dread and despair. He'll use his false imaginations to paint a picture of unrealistic disasters, and if you don't take those thoughts captive immediately in the name of Jesus, they will soon usher in with them a spirit of debilitating fear. Your heart consists of your mind, emotions, and will, therefore, as the Word of God says: *Guard your heart with all diligence* (Proverbs 4:23 NHEB).

Your heart is extremely vulnerable during difficult times and the enemy knows it, so be on your guard at all times against the onslaught of the evil one. Keep a close guard on where you allow it to go. Keep your mind in check, or your emotions will be sure to take over, and, before you know it, you'll be willfully doing and saying things you will later regret. Train your mind to dwell in places of safety and fight back against the evil thoughts of the Devil by quoting the faithful promises of God. They are your spiritual armor and firm anchor throughout the valley of deep darkness. Begin to write down God's promises and use them as your counter-strike when the enemy sends his fiery arrows of discouragement and defeat your way. They will be your most powerful weapons against him when disaster strikes.

Never forget that our God is a promise keeper, therefore we can stand on His promises as our faithful weapons against the evil ones.

For no matter how many promises God has made, they are "Yes" in

Christ. And so through him the "Amen" is spoken by us to the glory of God. (2 Corinthians 1:20)

The "amen" is spoken through Him---by us! Use God's promises like a weapon against the evil one. Again, God's Word reminds us that we don't war against people, but against Satan; the face of our enemy is Satan, not people! He's always trying to cut into our souls (mind, emotions, and will) by using those around us who are weak in their faith . . . they are his fertile fields for bringing discouragement. Often times they don't even realize they are being used by him to do it. Nonetheless, saved or unsaved, they are not the enemy, only his easy ploys. Never lose sight of the fact that the Devil is just like any bully—someone who's always trying to get the best of you by tearing you down. Don't let him do it, because whatever gets the best of you, takes the best *from* you.

And why does he do this? He's trying to distract you from the real battle and get you to lose your spiritual edge—your Christian witness before those who are watching your walk. Stay spiritually sharp by keeping your eyes on Him and by dwelling in His secret place. Discipline your mind to stay in His safe place, the shadow of His wings—Satan dare not come near that holy place of refuge!

For in the day of trouble he will keep me safe in his dwelling (Psalm 27:5).

Now, let's look at something else from a practical and spiritual perspective. When you get up in the morning, you put on your clothes for the day, right? You wouldn't think about going out naked where people could see you. Then why in the world would you go into battle without putting on the armor of God? Think about it: a good soldier never forgets to put on his full armor before heading into a war zone, and we shouldn't either. It's just that simple! Either armor up or get beat up . . . the choice is yours.

Now let's just stop right here for a moment so I can clarify a few things before we move on with more of God's insightful instructions. I hope you're not thinking, "She is so wise." Oh no, my friend, the only wise thing I did was follow God's leading. The only reason I'm so well versed on all these things is because I learned the hard way, by falling victim to almost every trap I've discussed in this book. And, believe me, it was only by the grace of God that I was set free from these traps. Let me say this right now: the only *wise heroes* in this story are Jesus Christ, Father God, and Holy Spirit, each of whom were my faithful companions who rescued me from all of these evil traps.

I will extol the Lord at all times; his praise will always be on my lips. I will glory in the Lord; let the afflicted hear and rejoice. Glorify the Lord with me; let us exalt his name together. I sought the Lord, and he answered me; he delivered me from all my fears. Those who look to him are radiant; their faces are never covered with shame. This poor man called, and the Lord heard him; he saved him out of all his troubles (Psalm 34:1-6).

I just had to take a moment and once again give all the praise and glory for these amazing victories to the One who made *all things possible*! You see, bringing glory to God is what compelled me to write this book. How could I not tell His story and bring honor to Him for all the goodness and faithfulness He showed to all of us during one of the most difficult times in our lives. As a matter of fact, I was inspired to do so after I read the story of Joshua's bravery and steadfastness to God throughout his life. God asked the Israelites to set up stones in the middle of the Jordan River as a reminder of what the LORD had done:

In the future, when your children ask you, 'What do these stones mean?' tell them that the flow of the Jordan was cut off before the ark of the covenant of the Lord. When it crossed the Jordan, the waters of the Jordan were cut off (Joshua 4:6-7).

Each battle plan and victory that I have written about in this book is my personal stone of remembrance for what God did in all of our lives during this difficult time of crossing over into our own Promised Land. Perhaps, one day, my grandchild will ask me why I wrote this book, and I can tell them to read these incredible stories of God's wisdom and faithfulness and then they too will know why I wrote it.

With that being said, let's move on to some more of God's wise counsel, the very wisdom of God that helped me and my family pass through the demon-possessed valley and cross over the raging rivers to our Promised Land.

Another strategy the Lord taught me to avoid being beaten up by the Devil was to get up extra early in the mornings so I would have time to dress myself properly for the battles that were sure to come that day. By that, I mean He showed me the importance of grabbing hold of my shield of faith, putting on my breastplate of righteousness, and picking up the sword of His Spirit, before heading out the door. Also, He doesn't want us to forget our helmet of salvation and the essential belt of truth that holds our armor all together. You've decided to join God's Army and participate with Him in the fight; this means that, just like any military soldier who joins the army, you can expect a fight somewhere during your day, especially if you're on the frontlines in a war zone . . . so be ready!

We're in a war all right, but let's not forget what kind of war it is—it's *spiritual*. That's why it's called spiritual warfare. And believe me, God is watching to see if His warriors are dressed and ready for the battle just like any good commander would be.

The eyes of the LORD are on the righteous, and his ears are attentive to their cry (Psalm 34:15).

Keep in mind, Satan is watching too. He sees your vulnerable nakedness when you forget to wear your spiritual armor and he knows it's the perfect time to launch another attack.

Be alert and of sober mind. Your enemy the devil prowls around like a roaring lion looking for someone to devour (1 Peter 5:8).

Has the Devil been prowling around in your mind today? Are you feeling defeated and afraid? Then think about where you've been dwelling. By that I mean, where have you willfully allowed your mind and emotions to go? As the Word says, be alert and sober minded; don't let him devour you by dwelling on his thoughts. Put up your shield of faith. Did you forget to put on some of your armor today? Did you leave your mind unguarded without your helmet of salvation? If so, reset your mind by quickly running back to your place of safety, then begin to dwell on the things above.

Set your minds on things above, not on earthly things (Colossians 3:2).

The Word of God tells us what mindset we should have. This is our safe place:

Finally, brothers and sisters, whatever is true, whatever is noble, whatever is right, whatever is pure, whatever is lovely, whatever is admirable—if anything is excellent or praiseworthy—think about such things (Philippians 4:8).

This is where our mind should dwell if we want to live in a place of victory throughout our day. Wars are won one battle at a time, and battles one day at a time. Therefore reset your mind and keep it set—the battle is in your mind! This is where the enemy attacks your emotions, speaking fear-filled words or bringing in false imaginations that feel like fiery arrows that invade your mind and try to overshadow God's words of hope. His defeating words steal our peace and joy and drain our spiritual strength.

In addition to all of these, hold up the shield of faith to stop the fiery arrows of the devil (Ephesians 6:16 NLT).

We must be ready to fight back at all times by being aware of his evil tactics. If we're going to fight back and block those fiery darts (evil thoughts), we need to have our shield up and our sword drawn! Spiritually speaking, we are blocking his flaming arrows and guarding our hearts. God's weapons of warfare are given to you to help you guard your heart. Again, that's your mind, will, and emotions.

You can easily see the condition of a person's heart based on their emotions and what comes out of their mouth. As their emotions run wild, you can hear their defeated words flowing out. And that is exactly what the enemy is listening for while he prowls about: he's watching and listening for those weak and vulnerable moments. I truly believe demons are drawn to us when they hear negative words of defeat coming out of our mouths. Why wouldn't they be? Those people are speaking their language, and they can't wait to join in on the conversation!

Be on your guard; stand firm in the faith; be courageous; be strong (1 Corinthians 16:13).

The Word of God tells us: *If you do not stand firm in your faith, you will not stand at all* (Isaiah 7:9). This word especially hits home when you're in the heat of the battle! Let's face it, our greatest weapons of warfare won't be there to protect us if we don't remember to put them on daily. Wear them as part of your daily clothing and then you'll be able to stand firm when the enemy attacks your mind. You'll be ready to fight back at the first onslaught of the enemy's fiery arrows, by speaking the Word of God in faith! Speak the Word as if you are talking face to face with the evil one—because you are! Speak it with the God-given authority that comes from Jesus.

Jesus said, *Look, I have given you authority over all the power of the enemy . . . Nothing will injure you* (Luke 10:19 NLT). These are the trusted words of our Savior, our commander-in-chief! We are His high-ranking officers, and we certainly have rank over the evil ones, because He has already defeated them and given all authority over them to us. We need to take Christ at His word and use our God-given high-ranking authority to defeat this enemy and stop allowing him to injure or defeat us with his negative thoughts and false imaginations.

When I first came back to Christ at the age of twenty-three, I didn't have a clue about any of this. Almost immediately after making a new commitment to follow Christ with all my heart, I found myself tormented in my mind with past sins. Because I knew nothing about oppressing demon spirits, I had no idea why this was happening. Nevertheless, they constantly accused me of my past sins, making me feel ashamed and unworthy of Christ's forgiveness and salvation. The truth was, they wanted to oppress my mind with defeating thoughts and keep me back from believing who I really was in Christ. That was their battle strategy to defeat me. Thank God, I was so grateful for Jesus' rescuing me that I was determined not to give up. In other words, my mind was set and there was no way I was going to betray my Savior. Again, Satan likes to get us when we are weak. Spiritually speaking, I was a newborn baby and barely getting started in my new Christian walk.

Those ol' evil ones are always trying to bombard our minds with negative thoughts that make us feel powerless and defeated, and hoping we won't realize who we really are. The last thing they want us to know or see is the spiritual powerhouses we really are through Christ! Praise God, from reading this book and hearing God's instructive words, you know better than that by now. You have learned how to invoke the power and authority of Jesus and command them to flee! When I finally learned what was truly happening to me, and the power and authority I had as a child of the Most High God, I spoke to those demons and said, "Demons, I command you to flee from me . . . in the name of Jesus!" Immediately after speaking those word, they took off running! I'll never forget that; it was as though I could feel them fleeing! Looking back now, although I didn't completely realize it at the time, I was fighting back by faith as I put up my mighty shield of faith and exercised my God-given authority over them.

Stand firm then, with the belt of truth buckled around your waist, with the breastplate of righteousness in place, and with your feet fitted with the readiness that comes from the gospel of peace. In addition to all this, take up the shield of faith, with which you can extinguish all the flaming arrows of the evil one (Ephesians 6:14-16).

Whenever accusing or worrisome thoughts ran through my mind, I'd ask myself right out loud, "Where am I dwelling? What am I thinking about? What am I doing that keeps stealing my joy and peace? What do I keep rehearsing over and over in my mind?" This personal inventory would help me to identify where I was dwelling . . . in the Devil's den!

Then I would immediately move out of that dwelling place by extinguishing all their flaming arrows by faith with the Word of God!

When Jesus found Himself in the Devil's den, He used the Word of God to resist him—*it is written . . .*

Asking myself those questions was my way of giving myself a good spiritual jolt. If you will get in a habit of asking yourself these questions too, I know it will be the jolt of spiritual electricity needed to reset your mind on things above and get you back to your dwelling place of safety too.

Remember, with others we need to be gentle, but sometimes with ourselves we need to be brutally honest. Listen to your own words and thoughts. See if you notice that fear is speaking way too loudly in your conversations with yourself and others. If so, then immediately turn things around by speaking words of faith and life. If you will guard your heart in this way and give honest answers to the questions I've suggested, I believe it will be a wonderful guide to help you determine the problem. Not only that, you will understand why fear and anxiety have gripped your mind and emotions . . . and what you need to do about it.

It seems as if women are always thinking about something. So pay very close attention to what you're thinking about at all times, especially when you've been injured by someone's words or actions. Is fear speaking or is faith speaking? If the answer is fear, then it's time to change the channel and reset the dial. Start to block the wrong thought waves by connecting to the right channel—God's channel. If you haven't been in the habit of doing this, it will take lots of practice at first. But eventually, if you will keep checking yourself in this area, it will lead you right back to the place of God's safety and refuge—right back into the shadow of His wings.

Lord Almighty, my King and my God. Blessed are those who dwell in your house (Psalm 84:3-4).

Restore us again, God our Savior (Psalm 85:4).

Never forget that the same overcoming power that raised Christ from the dead lives in you. Because Jesus won, you can choose, as a believer, to operate from a place of victory at all times. And if you do, your victory is assured!

Who will bring any charge against those whom God has chosen? . . . Who shall separate us from the love of Christ? Shall trouble or hardship or persecution . . . No, in all these things we are more than conquerors through him who loved us (Romans 8:33,35,37).

Yes, this is where we dwell—in Jesus' victory. He is standing in the Victor's Circle with a cloud of witnesses, just waiting for us to join in the fight with them. This is not only our place of victory, it's the only safe place from the destructive, accusing, and worrisome thoughts of our enemy.

I can't encourage you enough to stay alert and vigilant in this area, especially during your most vulnerable moments. Again, don't let the enemy blame you and don't rehearse the past hurts in your mind. Stop rehearsing it! Take those thoughts captive in Jesus' name! Declare those things that are not seen right now as though they are already done. We do this by believing and trusting the words and promises of God are true!

It is written, *the God who gives life to the dead and calls into being things that were not* (Romans 4:17). We are calling the promises of God into being. Yes, we are calling the dead bones back to life. We are calling God's plans, His dreams and destiny for our child's life into being.

Jesus said: *Very truly I tell you, the Son can do nothing by himself; he can do only what he sees his Father doing, because whatever the Father does the Son also does* (John 5:19-20). Things that are not yet seen! That's what we see our Lord and Savior doing. We see that while He was here on the earth, He was waiting and watching to see what the Father did next so He would know what to do. If we are going to operate in this way too, we must be like Jesus and watch for God's next move or battle plan. We're like those *whose hearts are set on pilgrimage* (Psalm 84:5). We may be in a physical world, but we're on a spiritual journey while we're here. That's why we must set our minds and keep them set—we cannot be double minded. In other words, we can't keep going back and forth in what we say and think if we want to be *more than conquerors through him who loved us* (Romans 8:37).

Again, as we see from reading these scriptures, we can't do anything by ourselves, but we can do whatever we see the Father doing, just like Jesus did. If we see God doing something in His Word, and He tells *us* to do the same thing, then with Him by our side, it *will* be done on earth as it is in heaven. On the other hand, we can see where a doubting, double-minded person is divided and unstable in his thoughts, conversely blocking their own ability to operate as Christ did. This mindset will keep them in the same old vicious circle of defeat, as they continue to go around and around the same old mountain.

Such a person is double-minded and unstable in all they do (James 1:8).

You can't say one minute, when you are feeling victorious, "I'm expecting and believing God for a great victory!" Then, in a moment of weakness, say, "I'm so worried. I just don't know what we are going to do if God doesn't come through for us." I doubt those defeated words are moving any mountains. Nor do they exalt God. Speak words of faith! It's a choice.

Choose you this day whom ye will serve (Joshua 24:15 KJV).

Again I say, whose report will you believe? The report of the evil one whispering (or shouting) in your ear or what the Word of God says about the matter?

Who has believed our message and to whom has the arm of the Lord been revealed? (Isaiah 53:1).

If you want God's powerful arm revealed in your life to move mightily *through* you into the direction of victory, then it will take unwavering faith that believes and trust Him explicitly! Especially when you are in the heat of the battle.

If you believe, you will receive whatever you ask for in prayer (Matthew 21:22).

Do you see the word *if* in that verse? God's Word comes with a condition or, you might say, a clause: you must *believe*! That's why it's extremely important you stay close to your loving Father God; that way you won't leave room for doubt to creep in and steal what He has promised you. I believe the enemy uses our very words against us to justify his attacks. He can look God right in the eye and say, "Their words agree with me . . . not You!" Our words are powerful, and if left unchecked, they can give the enemy an edge in the battle.

How does the Word of God say we overcome the evil one? *They triumphed over him by the blood of the Lamb and by the word of their testimony* (Revelation 12:11). Yes, the *word* of their testimony . . . overcoming, conquering words spoken by faith! So don't let evil thoughts consume you, and don't start speaking words of fear and doubt, but run to Him when you feel weary and vulnerable . . . cry out to Him on His mercy seat. Draw from His amazing mercy and grace. Start right there each morning before you get out of bed—before the Devil even knows you're awake. Speak words of faith while you're still lying in your bed! This is the perfect time to draw from His mercies, which He says are new every morning:

Through the Lord's mercies we are not consumed, because His compassions fail not. They are new every morning; great is Your faithfulness (Lamentations 3:22-23 NKJV).

Don't dwell on thoughts from the enemy and let them consume you; instead, fill yourself up with His virtues and His new mercies first thing every morning. This was another battle strategy the Lord gave me, and one of my best weapons of warfare for getting a jump on the enemy! From the moment I realized I was waking up, before I even opened my eyes, I would lift my hands up high toward heaven and begin to thank my Lord for His new mercies that day. Then I would draw from the fruit of His Spirit, filling my spirit up with His love, joy, peace, patience, kindness, goodness, gentleness, and self-control. Yes, the very virtues of God are mine and yours for the asking, simply because we are His children. Feed on that fruit first thing every morning and watch how it sets your mind on the things above. As I did this each morning, I soon discovered I had a new kind of supernatural nourishment for my soul and new spiritual strength I never had before.

But the fruit of the Spirit is love, joy, peace, forbearance, kindness, goodness, faithfulness, gentleness and self-control (Galatians 5:22-23).

I can't encourage you enough to do this. Let His glorious virtues flow into your spirit first thing every morning. What an easy and great way to fill your hungry spirit and refresh your thirsty weary soul . . . with the fresh, bountiful, sweet fruit of His Spirit.

After you finish doing that, get up and run to His Word for a fresh message from Him for the day. Jesus said, *Blessed are those who hunger and thirst for righteousness, for they will be filled* (Matthew 5:6). Think about it: you wouldn't go through the day without eating, would you? If you did, you would soon become weak and weary. Oh no, we wouldn't think of doing that. When we hear our belly growl, we get right up and get something to satisfy the hunger. This same concept applies when we don't eat (the bread of life) from the Word of God. We become weak and drained *spiritually*, until we feed on the Word. We need to nourish our hungry souls and refresh our thirsty spirits by spending time eating from the bread of life and drinking from His well of living water.

Then Jesus declared, "I am the bread of life. Whoever comes to me will never go hungry, and whoever believes in me will never be thirsty" (John 6:35).

I want to encourage you to get up early, that way you won't be rushed out of His presence while in worship. The Lord impressed upon me during this critical time to get up an hour and a half earlier in the mornings just to spend time with Him before I got ready for my day.

Trust me when I say, I'm not a morning person, so I would head straight for my coffee pot first. After giving myself a few minutes to wake up while drinking my coffee and meditating on His goodness, I would go straight to His Word and then on into prayer. Often times I would get so caught up entering His courts with shouts of praise and thanksgiving that I would lose complete track of the time. Before I knew it, my joyful time with the Lord was going on much longer than I realized.

If you have a work schedule, or somewhere you must be on time, I would encourage you to set an alarm; that way you won't be distracted by worrying about the time. Because this is such an important and special time with God, you will want your mind completely free to dwell in His presence.

Satan always tries to interrupt this important time, so put up safe guards by turning off your cell phone and doing whatever it takes to focus completely on Him. I don't know about you, but oftentimes my to-do list will try to stifle my worship and prayer time. Never forget that all prayer is warfare! At first, it seemed like he just loved to use this list to remind me of all the things I couldn't forget to do that day. And trust me, as a busy realtor, I had plenty of important details on my to-do list. The best remedy I found was to thank him for reminding me, write it down if I thought I needed to, and then tell him to, *Get out of my prayer room*! Your prayer room is your *war* room . . . how dare he cross that frontline!

Another distraction all of us tend to struggle with is a wandering mind. My remedy to this problem was to pray right out loud. Praying out loud keeps you engaged in your thoughts and keeps you focused on the Lord. If this feels strange, look at it this way: you're sitting down with a close friend and you're having a meaningful and purposeful conversation. Remember who you are talking to: Jesus, your great Counselor, Helper, and best Friend. He loves the sound of your voice, and, as your best friend, He wants to hear your concerns and answer your requests.

I no longer call you servants, because a servant does not know his master's business. Instead, I have called you friends, for everything that I learned from my Father I have made known to you (John 15:15).

Think about what the Lord is saying here. He's saying, *because I consider you My best friend, I'm comfortable telling you My Father's secrets.* He Who dwells in the Secret Place of the Most High wants to tell you the Father's secrets. What! Now that's something we need to know. As a matter of fact, I believe the battle instructions He gave me during this time were His secret weapons of warfare against the Devil.

That said, we need to be careful who we tell our secrets to. Not everyone is a true, dependable, caring friend. But you can tell Jesus anything and everything, and He will tell you what the Father has to say about the matter; either through His written Word or straight into your mind. Again, we never know how the Lord will speak, but He wants you to know He hears your prayers and, as a result, He will answer them if you will seek Him with your whole heart.

You will seek me and find me when you seek me with all your heart (Jeremiah 29:13).

For all one knows, God might require His earthly soldier to help with the problems of this world, so listen and watch carefully and follow His lead—do what you see the Father doing.

And since we know he hears us when we make our requests, we also know that he will give us what we ask for (1 John 5:15 NLT).

Only the Father knows how to make everything work out perfectly for our good and the good of our loved ones. Learn to listen closely as Jesus tells you about God's secret plans, that way you can defeat the Devil and overcome your problems. Abide in Him and take time to hear from your Lord, for He has the faithful answers. Don't just sit with Him telling Him what your problems are. He already knows them anyway. But learn to listen and watch for His instructions.

Abide in me, and I in you. As the branch cannot bear fruit by itself, unless it abides in the vine, neither can you, unless you abide in me (John

15:4 ESV).

Another way of looking at these distractions would be from a friend's perspective: if you were doing all the talking and never gave your friend a chance to give you their thoughts, they probably wouldn't feel very important. Also, if you kept letting your mind wander and you weren't engaged in the conversation with them, that wouldn't make them feel special either.

I'll never forget the time I called a dear Christian friend of mine after a heart wrenching experience in my life. As I poured out my broken heart to her on the phone, I noticed she wasn't as engaged or concerned as I thought she would be, when, suddenly, I heard crunching noises on the other end. I'll never forget how grieved that made me feel, as though my heart had been betrayed and I wasn't as important to her as I thought I was. Not only that, it was as if my heart-breaking story was the entertainment and she was having popcorn to go with it. How sad.

Jesus is your best friend, and, trust me when I say, you have His full attention at all times. Not to mention His heartfelt concern on the other end of the line.

After you finish praying, always take a few moments to listen for His still, small voice by sitting quietly in His presence. He will talk to you. If you have a problem hearing from God in this way, ask Him to give you spiritual ears to hear His voice. Remember, Jesus said, *My sheep hear my voice, and I know them, and they follow me* (John 10:27 KJV). This is a very important and serious matter, because if you don't learn to train your ears to hear His voice, you may find yourself listening to the wrong voice—Satan's!

When I'm not sure if I'm hearing the Lord clearly, I often ask Him to clear my spiritual ears to hear Him. If it's a very important decision I need to make, I will even test the spirit to make sure it's God's perfect will for me. As I said before, I have never heard the Lord speak audibly like some people have, but, I do hear Him speaking very clearly in my mind.

If you're not sure if it's God's voice speaking to you, then I would encourage you to test the words by putting out a fleece. As a matter of fact, if you are being told or encouraged to do something by an *individual* that you aren't sure about, I would definitely tell you to test the spirit, especially if it's in regard to something that would alter your life or someone else's life considerably.

Beloved, do not believe every spirit, but test the spirits, whether they are of God; because many false prophets have gone out into the world (1 John 4:1 NKJV).

One way to test the spirit is to put out a fleece. To better understand what this means, let me show you in God's Word where He confirmed a man's prayer using a fleece:

The story starts off with Gideon being visited by the angel of the Lord. The angel of the Lord greets him with these uplifting and encouraging words: *The LORD is with you, mighty warrior* (Judges 6:12). However, Gideon didn't see himself with the same spiritual eyes that the angel of the Lord did and, as a result, his reaction was one of defeat. Gideon responded by saying: *if the Lord is with us, why has all this happened to us? Where are all his wonders that our ancestors told us about . . . But now the Lord has abandoned us and given us into the hand of Midian* (Judges 6:13).

Then Gideon went on with his complaining and doubting, even after the angel told him he was the one chosen by God to deliver the Israelite nation: *"How can I save Israel? My clan is the weakest in Manasseh, and I am the least in my family." The Lord answered, "I will be with you, and you will strike down all the Midianites, leaving none alive"* (Judges 6:15-16).

As we can see from Gideon's response, he must have struggled with deceptive, evil, oppressing thoughts too. He had lost sight of his God-given identity and saw himself much like the enemy wants us to see ourselves. Consequently, he found himself lacking in the confidence to do what he was born to do.

Nevertheless, at this point in the story we see where Gideon begins to see himself differently. He starts to believe the angel of the Lord and finally decides to take him at his word. But not before confirming the word with his God.

Gideon knew this was a huge deal, not only for him, but for the army of Israel that he would lead into battle. Gideon wanted to be sure that this person was an angel of the Lord, and that his instruction was the will of his God, before he involved the entire army of Israel. Not a bad idea if you ask me!

So Gideon went before the Lord in prayer to ask Him to confirm that this was His will for him and the nation of Israel.

Gideon said to God, "If you will save Israel by my hand as you have promised—look, I will place a wool fleece on the threshing floor. If there is dew only on the fleece and all the ground is dry, then I will know that you will save Israel by my hand, as you said." And that is what happened. Gideon rose early the next day; he squeezed the fleece and wrung out the dew—a bowlful of water (Judges 6:36-38).

Although God answered Gideon's request by giving him a sign using the fleece, Gideon was still lacking in self-confidence and afraid to lead the army of Israel into battle. Therefore, he prayed to the Lord once again and said, *"Do not be angry with me. Let me make just one more request. Allow me one more test with the fleece, but this time make the fleece dry and let the ground be covered with dew." That night God did so. Only the fleece was dry; all the ground was covered with dew* (Judges 6:39-40).

God is so patient with us. Often times, throughout my weary journey, I could relate to Gideon's fears and doubts. Sometimes, while you're in the heat of the battle, when things seem to be getting worse instead of better, you can't help but to wonder, *where is God? Has he abandoned us? Where are the powerful mighty works that I used to see Him do in my life? Have I fallen from grace?*

Let's face it: when you're in the middle of the petrifying, demon-possessed valley and all you can see around you are the stressful, heart-wrenching circumstances, the last thing you think about yourself is *what a mighty warrior of God I am!* Oh no, I can't judge Gideon because I have been there myself.

I'm so thankful that God is patient with us just like he was with Gideon. We must wear Him out sometimes. I'm sure I did, and still do. As a matter of fact, I put out my own fleece in the fall of 2014, after the Lord spoke to me one day while I was simply walking through my home. Although I'd heard Him very clearly, I had a Gideon moment as thoughts started running wildly through my head: *Who am I? I'm the least likely person to have such an honor bestowed on me. And besides, I'm not a young person anymore.* Nevertheless, God's words, "I want you to be ordained," needed to be confirmed.

As a matter of fact, He didn't really even ask me, He just told me what He wanted. Without argument, I simply said, "Lord, I don't know of any schools in this local area, or where to start, but if this is what you want me to do, then confirm it by putting a school in my path." In the meantime, I didn't do anything to help God along, so to speak.

Three days later, I was riding with a dear Christian brother of mine and I asked him the question I always like to ask true believers: "What's God doing in your life right now?" Without looking up from the steering wheel, he said, "Me and God are fighting right now." I responded by saying, "You know you're going to lose, right? May I ask what in the world you are fighting with God about?"

"Our church is starting a ministry school," he said, "and my pastor wants me to enroll."

I could hardly believe my ears. It just so happened that I was the realtor who had worked hand in hand with his pastor for the past three years while he and his congregation looked for a new church building. His pastor and I had become dear friends because of our close working relationship. Instantly, I realized God had just confirmed my call or (fleece).

Without speaking another word, I turned to my friend and said, "Well, brother, it looks like I will be in that school with you. When does it start?"

"Five days from now."

Needless to say, the rest is history. I was ordained four years later on January 21. 2018.

So now when someone says to me, "I don't believe in women ministers," I simply say, "It wasn't my idea." The Word of God says, *There is neither Jew nor Gentile, neither slave nor free, nor is there male and female, for you are all one in Christ Jesus* (Galatians 3:28).

Yes, I have been a Gideon more times than I would like to admit. There were several times in my dark, bleak valley days that I too felt like a weak, powerless woman with absolutely no significance, just like Gideon. Even so, it was during those times that I kept moving forward by faith and doing what the Lord told me to do, although I was often petrified with fear. Sometimes you just have to do it afraid! That's the definition of courage . . . doing something even though you're afraid.

Another important thing I learned throughout my many difficult battles was, when the Lord gives you the answer and says, *Go, I will be with you. You will strike down and destroy your enemy*, it's time to *move out!* We see this in the fortieth year of the Israelites' captivity, when the Lord spoke to them and said, *You have stayed long enough at this mountain. Break camp and advance* (Deuteronomy 1:6-7). In essence, God was saying, "Your wilderness season is over, and it's time to MOVE!" 'You have dwelt here long enough. Time to move on into your promised destiny."

Have you stayed long enough at your mountain? Then it's time to get up and start advancing towards your Promised Land! Do whatever the Lord tells you to do. Do it afraid if you have to, even if it makes no sense at the time. Again, you do this by keeping your focus and eyes on

Him. Use your spiritual eyes to see yourself as He does—a mighty warrior of God! You *will* win, no matter how insurmountable the odds of winning may seem . . . that's how God is glorified in your life! *Do not be terrified; do not be afraid of them. The LORD your God, who is going before you, will fight for you* (Deuteronomy 1:29-30).

How many demons are you facing in the valley today? How many battles have you fought in? Remember, the Lord not only promises to go with you, but to give you His strength during those difficult times, to keep you advancing. So rise up and draw from the Lord's supernatural strength and see how quickly your natural strength will return as He upholds you with His righteous right hand.

So do not fear, for I am with you; do not be dismayed, for I am your God. I will strengthen you and help you; I will uphold you with my righteous right hand (Isaiah 41:10).

Don't forget that you are never alone in your battles; the God of Heaven's Armies is fighting right beside you, along with His warring angel army! Again, always remember to dwell in God's presence where His shadow protects and surrounds you. He says, *Be strong and courageous. Do not be afraid or terrified because of them, for the Lord your God goes with you; he will never leave you nor forsake you* (Deuteronomy 31:6).

We must start to see ourselves as God sees us and never forget that *He is there!* The Hebrews calls Him *Jehovah Shammah*, which means the Lord is there. Unfortunately, if you don't believe this truth, you may be prone to believe the lies the enemy has to say about you too. Consequently, you will not accomplish the amazing things God has planned for you to do. Think about it: how will you ever be able to fight for yourself and your loved ones if you don't truly believe He is with you and fighting for you? He is also called *Jehovah Elohim*—the strong and mighty One who fights our battles for us!

Jesus replied, "Truly I tell you, if you have faith and do not doubt, not only can you do what was done to the fig tree, but also you can say to this mountain, 'Go, throw yourself into the sea,' and it will be done" (Matthew 21:21). It's time to tell that mountain (or stronghold) to get down! Any thought, action, or even something another person has said about you or your loved one that is allowed to exalt itself above what God says about you or them could become a stronghold in your mind . . . cast it down!

We demolish arguments and every pretension that sets itself up against the knowledge of God, and we take captive every thought to make it obedient to Christ (2 Corinthians 10:5).

Yes, it's time to demolish some thoughts before they become strongholds again; by taking every thought captive in Jesus' name. This is God's way of helping us to overcome bad beliefs or negative thoughts. Take them captive and make them conform and be obedient to what Christ says. Immediately, say right out loud, "That's not a God thought, and I won't dwell on it another minute. I take that thought captive in Jesus' name and cast it down!"

Also, the Word of God tells us to cast down wrong imaginations.

Casting down imaginations, and every high thing that exalteth itself against the knowledge of God (2 Corinthians 10:5 KJV).

If we keep giving over to the false imaginations of the Devil by dwelling on the things he wants us to dwell on, we will soon find ourselves paralyzed by his spirit of fear. The scripture referenced above tells us what to do with those false imaginations—cast them down! Just as Satan was cast down from heaven by God, we have the same power and authority to cast down his evil thoughts and remove them from our minds. If we want to see our victory come to pass, then at some point, like Gideon, we must determine whether or not we believe the report of the Lord, and act on what He is telling us to do.

Who hath believed our report? and to whom is the arm of the LORD revealed? (Isaiah 53:1 KJV).

If God calls us mighty warriors and great men and women of valor, then we need to start seeing ourselves as He does. We need to take our rightful positions. It's okay to be bold and confident in who you are in Jesus, especially in the face of the enemy. That's why the Lord keeps building you up and strengthening you—He's trying to get you to understand that's who you *really* are in Him!

The enemy wants to keep us looking back at who we once were. That's why he keeps reminding us of all our failures and past sins. It's part of his strategic plan by which he achieves his overall goal to destroy us and our loved ones. Never lose sight of the fact that he's the bully of all bullies, and his hate-filled, destructive words are spoken in our ears to deliberately tear us down mentally and spiritually. And when does he come at us the hardest? When we are struggling with our circumstances and feeling spiritually weak. That's when he tries his best to finish us off, by making us feel even more defeated and powerless.

If we don't fight back, even during our weakest state, we may be deceived and inadvertently forfeit our true identity to the enemy. Let's face it: the Devil already knows who you are in Christ Jesus, and he knows too that you have *all* authority and power over him. He's just hoping *you* don't know it!

The Lord of Heaven's armies says: *No, in all these things we are more than conquerors through him who loved us. For I am convinced that neither death nor life, neither angels nor demons, neither the present nor the future, nor any powers, neither height nor depth, nor anything else in all creation, will be able to separate us from the love of God that is in Christ Jesus our Lord* (Romans 8:37-39).

Paul is talking to the people of God in this scripture. God says you are more than a conqueror, and nothing in all of creation can change that fact, nor can it separate you from His love. Paul was completely convinced. Now, my friend, you need to be completely convinced too. The Lord has already made up His mind and settled the matter. Now it's time for you to make up yours!

Think about it. Would you want your child to look only at his or her failures and let that be how they identify themselves? If they did, they would never rise up and fulfill God's destiny for their life. They would live a defeated life ruled by the prince of this world and his demons. I say with Paul, *no, in all these things we are more than conquerors through him who loved us!*

King David said, *The Lord is the stronghold of my life—of whom shall I be afraid?* (Psalm 27:1). The Lord offers help for today and hope for our future. Unwavering confidence is the antidote for fear! Stare down your enemy with unwavering confidence in Christ and tell him, "I am not afraid of you." Say it right out loud! Say it until you know it to be true and Satan knows it too!

I recently heard a story that really put all of this into perspective for me, and its message is very clear. In this story, a man arrived in heaven and asked St. Peter, "Who was the mightiest general who ever lived?" St. Peter pointed to a man in heaven whom this man had known on earth. He said, "St. Peter, that can't be. I knew that man on earth and he was just a laborer." St. Peter replied, "I know, but if he would have done what God purposed for him to do in his life, he would have been the mightiest general to ever live!"

I know this was just a made up story, but the message is relatable. He missed it! I don't want to miss out on what God called me to be. Unfulfilled potential, that's what we should fear most in our lives.

Could it be that God has put you through this test in order to train you? Perhaps He placed in you all the potential you would ever need to become one of His greatest generals. Nevertheless, you will never know unless you step forward and follow His leading. Then you will become all that He intended you to be.

May we never forget that we are the apple of His eye! He protects us as we walk through the howling wilderness of this dark, evil valley. His wings are spread over us all the time, just like a mother eagle overspreads her young. She even carries them upon her wings, as does the Lord His people. There will be times during the storm that you will feel yourself soaring, but you know it's not on your own strength or power—that's when you realize He is carrying you upon His wings.

In a desert land he found him, in a barren and howling waste. He shielded him and cared for him; he guarded him as the apple of his eye, like an eagle that stirs up its nest and hovers over its young, that spreads its wings to catch them and carries them aloft (Deuteronomy 32:10,11).

That's the God I know!

The Word of God tells us that Peter's shadow healed people.

People brought the sick into the streets and laid them on beds and mats so that at least Peter's shadow might fall on some of them as he passed by (Acts 5:15).

I may be wrong about this because there's no biblical reference to back up my theory, but I believe the shadow that accompanied Peter's shadow was none other than the shadow of Almighty God! If my theory is true, then we know Peter walked very closely with his Lord, right in the shadow of His wings.

Peter understood the unshakable power and strength that could only be found in the dwelling place of his Lord—the shadow of the Almighty God. My friend, I want to encourage you to try with all your strength and might to live right there every single day throughout this war. Don't wait until you have the final victory to rejoice, but rejoice now, knowing your victory is certain as you trust in Jesus Christ, your forever overcoming Lord and Redeemer.

For in the day of trouble he will keep me safe in his dwelling (Psalm 27:5).

10

Speak Words of Life—Not Death!

The Spirit himself testifies with our spirit that we are God's children
(Romans 8:16).

When God speaks directly to our minds, the Holy Spirit within us testifies to our spirit what the Father is saying. Some call this a witness of the Spirit. On one of my darkest days, the Lord very clearly spoke directly to my mind and said, *Speak words of life, not death, and declare My promises. Speak to the obstacles and tell them to move. Speak to the situation. My power is within you; you have the power to speak and declare that mountain be removed!*

According to the Word of God, *the tongue has the power of life and death, and those who love it will eat its fruit* (Proverbs 18:21). The Lord was reminding me that His supernatural power lives inside of me. He was also showing me how to call it forth by speaking His words of life: *For the word of God is alive and active. Sharper than any double-edged sword* (Hebrews 4:12).

Those powerful instructions He spoke to me that day never left the forefront of my mind from then on. Their importance can't be stressed enough. Basically, He was saying, *The same power that raised Me from the grave lives inside of you, daughter! You have everything you need to win this war living right inside of you—Holy Spirit!*

Talk about potential! God's Word is alive and active and living right inside of us! His Spirit abides within us at all times, He's just waiting for us to activate it by using words of faith. I believe God was letting me know the power His Word holds when it's spoken by a true believer through faith. He was saying, *Speak My Word, because My Word is My breath and the power to defeat and destroy the demons that would try to take you down!*

Think about it: God breathed on the dead, dry bones and brought them to life, and you can't speak one word without using your breath. And He breathed into you the breath of life on the day you were born.

The Word says, *And then the lawless one will be revealed, whom the Lord Jesus will overthrow with the breath of his mouth and destroy by the splendor of his coming* (2 Thessalonians 2:8). That means we have to say it right out loud, because just thinking it in our minds doesn't require any breath. I must admit, the day that this instructive word came, I felt completely discouraged and defeated. But God, in His great mercy, was trying to encourage me to GET UP and GET MOVING once again. He was saying, *Start using what I have already given you!*

I knew this was a fresh new strategy. There would be no more just going through the motions. From that moment on, I spoke words of life. One thing I knew for certain, if I was ever going to live in a place of victory on a daily basis, I needed to do my part and rise up every day declaring the victory with the faith-filled words of my breath. Once again, God was teaching me how to participate in the war and *live in the victory—by faith!*

My circumstances may not have changed immediately, but my attitude did.

Yes, we were still in the dark, scary valley, but I was now even more determined than ever before to get on though that gross darkness. And I knew it was time to start flying by faith over that storm.

I decided to reset my mind, once again, on God's Word and His promises. It was time to *mount up with wings as eagles* (Isaiah 40:31

KJV), and, thanks be to God, by that time I knew how to mount up on those wings and fly. Although I was very weary in the battle that day, God was reminding me of the power He had given me to keep moving forward. That power was in my own breath, and, because of that, I had the ability to speak to any obstacle that got in my way. With that new weapon in hand, I spoke that day to what seemed like an unmovable obstacle and said, *Get down mountain; my victory is waiting on the other side!*

What are you facing today in the dark valley? Does it look like a mountain that can't be moved? If so, then look it square in the face and with the breath God breathed into you on the day He gave you life tell it to move! Get down, mountain! The Lord of Heaven's Army and His earthly warrior are coming through! My friend, it's time to prophesy once again! It's time to start speaking the Word of the Lord by faith, believing His *word* will go and do what it was sent to do.

Later on in my journey, while I was praying for my son, the Lord spoke to me once again and said, *Charlotte, you have prayed every prayer for your son, and you have declared every declaration over him. Now let go and let the Word go and do what it was sent to do!*

That day, I had a deeper understanding of what the Lord was saying to me, and I knew once again He was giving me another powerful kingdom secret . . . or battle strategy. It was time to let go of my son, spiritually speaking, and trust the Word of God to perform and do in him what I had already asked it to do. We see this in Isaiah, where God is telling His servant how His word operates in the spiritual realm.

So is my word that goes out from my mouth: It will not return to me empty, but will accomplish what I desire and achieve the purpose for which I sent it (Isaiah 55:11).

That day, I released my son completely into God's sovereign care, and, with that, I released the Word of God to go forth in his life and achieve the purpose for which God created that young man. The Psalmist said, *He sent His word, and healed them, and delivered them from their destructions* (Psalm 107:20 KJV).

From that time on, I started to pray for my son in a very different way. I would say, *Word of God, go forth and do what you were sent to do, according to the Father's perfect will for his life. Do it exceedingly and abundantly beyond what I could ever hope, think, or even imagine!*

The Word of God tells us that God is watching over His word, He is making sure it fulfills His purpose for sending it. We see this in the Lord's response to His servant:

The Lord said to me, "You have seen correctly, for I am watching to see that my word is fulfilled." (Jeremiah 1:12).

Remember, God's ways are not our ways.

As the heavens are higher than the earth, so are my ways higher than your ways and my thoughts than your thoughts (Isaiah 55:9).

He is God Almighty, and we need to learn to operate in the spiritual realm, according to the way He operates, if we want to see the same miracles they saw in the days of old. I took God at His word that day and I can truly say, soon after that day, I started seeing the miraculous take place in my son's life. It wasn't long after I released that boy and prayed that prayer that I noticed drastic changes taking place in my son's spiritual life. It was as if I'd loosed the hand of God and bound the powers of hell in a way I could never have imagined! Oh yes, the Word of the Lord was active in his life in a whole new way, and it was something amazing to witness!

This is why we need to use God's Word and speak boldly to those obstacles that come into our children's lives . . . and into our own lives too! When fear and anxiety try to come in like a flood, we need to raise up a standard against them by commanding with all the power and authority of heaven, *Fear and anxiety, hear the Word of the Lord and flee in Jesus' name! Doubt and unbelief, hear the Word of the Lord and flee! In Jesus' name I command you!* Send the Word of God forth and release it—it will do what it was sent to do. God will watch over that word to make sure it achieves what it was sent to do. The evidence will soon be seen as the peace of God returns to you after sending His word and releasing it to destroy the spirits of fear and anxiety that were invading your soul.

When the enemy shall come in like a flood, the Spirit of the Lord shall lift up a standard against him (Isaiah 59:19 KJV).

His Word is the standard against the evil one, and you just sent a more powerful flood forth the very moment you spoke it with the breath of your mouth! That's why it's so vitally important that we learn how to operate in the spiritual realm. We have the power within our breath to bind the powers of hell and loose the power of God by speaking words of life over our spiritually dead child or loved one. Jesus said, *Truly I tell you, whatever you bind on earth will be bound in heaven, and whatever you loose on earth will be loosed in heaven* (Matthew 18:18). This is God's spiritual way of doing things.

Now that you have a better understand of how God operates in the spirit realm, maybe it's time to let go of your loved one, too, and exchange the dreams and destiny you have in mind for them for God's dreams and destiny that *He* has in mind for them. I'll never regret the day I exchanged my dreams for His. That day was one of my finest moments, as I completely surrendered my son to my magnificent God! As I said before, from that moment on, I saw the miraculous begin to take place in his life.

***

Did you know that fear and faith are actually very much alike? Fear is believing something bad is going to happen. Faith is believing something good is going to happen. Can you see where both faith and fear **believe** something is going to happen?

The three Hebrew captives, who were thrown into the blazing, fiery furnace because they weren't willing to bow down to the king's idol, spoke faith-filled words of life. They said, *"If we are thrown into the*

*blazing furnace, the God we serve is able to deliver us from it, and he
will deliver us from Your Majesty's hand. But even if he does not, we
want you to know, Your Majesty, that we will not serve your gods or
worship the image of gold you have set up." Then Nebuchadnezzar was
furious with Shadrach, Meshach and Abednego, and his attitude toward
them changed. He ordered the furnace heated seven times hotter than
usual* (Daniel 3:17-19).

It's what you *believe* that you speak in your darkest hour, when
everything is on the line—even your life. Those young men were
determined to stand in faith and not dishonor their faithful God by
bowing to the pressure and speaking words of doubt and defeat, let alone
by bowing down to another god. I love where they said, *the God we
serve is able! But even if he does not . . .*

Now that's faith in action!

Oh yes, our God is able. But how many will lay it all down and still
trust Him, even if He doesn't come through in a way they expected Him
to? Even unto death! The Word of God goes on in this story to tell how
God richly rewarded their faith by showing up and rescuing them from
the fiery furnace. You see, God was already there. He is Jehovah
Shammah! I would love to have seen the proud papa look on Father
God's face that day. I hope I can make Him as proud as they did every
day of my life. I want God to beam with delight because of my
unwavering faith in Him.

Just like the evil king in this story, Satan is always trying to turn up
the heat when we won't bow to his spirit of fear. The Word of God calls
fear a spirit:

*For God hath not given us the spirit of fear; but of power, and of love,
and of a sound mind* (2 Timothy 1:7 KJV).

Don't make room for the spirit of fear. Notice the lowercase letter s?
We know from that alone it's a lower spirit. Remember, what you make
room for, you empower. If you make room for fear, then you are

empowering it. FEAR is F-false E-evidence A-appearing R-real. Don't allow fearful thoughts to come into your mind. Don't empower it by entertaining it. And try to *never* speak words of fear—speak words of life! Please stop making room for this spirit that is not of God, but of Satan.

Many people don't understand the affect fear has on their soul. Fear brings anxiety, and anxiety, left unchecked, brings depression. Anxiety comes from the inability to change or do something about a situation we have no control over. Trust me when I say, I fought with this demon of fear firsthand throughout my journey in the dark valley. And don't think he stopped trying even after the war was over either. Oh no, fear is a never-ending tide of emotions you are sure to face while down in the valley. My way of handling this evil spirit was to keep it in check by saying what the three Hebrew boys said: *The God I serve is able to deliver us from your hand old Devil . . . But even if He doesn't, I won't bow to you, demon spirit of fear!*

The fact is, the Devil can't get the best of you if he doesn't have anything on you. If you've surrendered everything to the Lord with all your heart, then that old trick won't work anymore.

He's just sitting there trying to think up some fearful thought to whisper in your ear. He says, *Aha! I'll get her with this fearful thought!* But when you stand in unrelenting faith, those thoughts from the Devil just bounce right off you. Can you imagine how deflating that is to him?

Whenever he'd try to whisper fearful thoughts to me, I would say right out loud, "But not today, Devil! Today we're all doing great!" That's why we need to live only one day at a time. The truth is, we aren't guaranteed tomorrow, only today. Stay in the present, and it really will become a present—every day is a gift from God.

Do not gloat over me, my enemy! Though I have fallen, I will rise. Though I sit in darkness, the Lord will be my light. (Micah 7:8)

The prophet Micah had the right attitude when he wrote that

scripture.

As the saying goes, our attitude determines our altitude. When trying to soar above the storms of life, our attitude is extremely important if we are going to soar in the higher altitudes. If you want to soar above the storm with the Lord, you must have a winning attitude and a willingness to get back up and fight. *Though I have fallen, I will rise!*

Did you know what comes out of your mouth has the power to create? According to the Word of God it does. That means we can create a hostile environment all around us, even within our own spirit, by using hateful and negative words or even just by dwelling on those kinds of thoughts. The enemy uses our own words to stir up anxiety, fear, and stress. We must learn to use self-control and rule over negative thoughts and choose to speak words of life by the power of God's Spirit living inside of us—it's a conscience choice. Not to mention an ongoing effort on our behalf. Go ahead and quote God's Word and do what you know is right, even if you don't feel like it at the time. Feelings are emotions that have a way of settling down very quickly when you do it God's way. That's why the Word says: *A gentle answer turns away wrath, but a harsh word stirs up anger* (Proverbs 15:1).

When you learn to use life-giving words on a regular basis, they will keep you in the right *attitude* that is needed in order to fly in the higher *altitudes*. That's when we start to notice we're soaring peacefully above the storm that has settled over the dark valley below. Oh yes, when our circumstances say, "You should be falling apart right now!" yet you have this unshakable peace, know that God's wind is under your wings . . . He's up to something, and all you need to do is keep on soaring effortlessly.

The truth is, quoting God's Word without applying faith to it can wear you out. It's like a bird that's constantly flapping its wings and never learning to soar with the wind. But once we learn to walk by faith and not by sight, we begin to soar effortlessly above the storm with the wind in our sails. It really doesn't matter what's going on in the valley below when you're in the higher altitudes; the sun is always shining above the clouds.

***

Remember earlier when I said your words have creative power? Watch what you say—the world was spoken into existence:

And God said, "let there be light," and there was light (Genesis 1:3).

Now that's creative power!

Be very careful what you create with the words of your mouth. Remember to always be mindful about what you could be speaking into existence in your own circumstances. Take a minute and think about what's been coming out of your mouth lately. Can you see where you need to make some changes in order to soar above your storm?

As I encouraged you before, be brutally honest with yourself. Are you speaking the good, creative, powerful things of God? Or are you moaning and complaining while using negative, defeating words and attitudes that give the enemy the upper hand? If so, you are giving him every right to torment you. Think about what kind of environment you have just created with those words. Are you creating an environment that draws the enemy in and lets him know you are vulnerable for an attack? Trust me, Satan is listening to what you say. And don't forget, God is listening too!

The eyes of the LORD are everywhere, keeping watch on the wicked and the good (Proverbs 15:3).

Again, if you're bent on victory, then start quoting His Word and standing on His promises that are "yes and amen!" We say amen to the Word of God in agreement with the Lord.

Oh, we *must* get this! Who speaks the amen? *We do!* And what does that amen mean? It means *so be it, according to what the Word of the Lord has spoken!* When you say amen, you are confirming that the word that was spoken is truth. That's why your pastor loves it when the congregation shouts out amen while he's preaching. He knows you are coming into agreement with the Word of God. Jesus said, *Again, truly I tell you that if two of you on earth agree about anything they ask for, it will be done for them by my Father in heaven* (Matthew 18:19).

There is power when we come into agreement with someone. Consequently, if we aren't careful about what we say, we will come into agreement with the enemy of our soul and allow him to create utter chaos in our lives by speaking words of defeat and death . . . right through our own mouths. Remember God's Word says what's in our hearts comes out through our mouths:

A good man brings good things out of the good stored up in his heart, and an evil man brings evil things out of the evil stored up in his heart. For the mouth speaks what the heart is full of (Luke 6:45).

As I said before, sometimes we only need to listen to what is coming out of our mouths to know where our hearts are! The bottom line is this: it's up to us to come into agreement with the Word of God and allow Him to change our hearts and attitude. If we notice that we have been speaking words of death, we need to confess it to the Lord and ask Him to forgive us. Then we must repent of what we've been doing by simply stopping it! Lastly, give those words of death to God and let Him wash them in the blood of Jesus and cancel the death sentence that was spoken forth. Admittedly, I'm well versed on this subject, because I too have been in that heart examination room before Almighty God confessing my sins in this area.

Speak words of life, my friend! Don't beat yourself up for the times you've spoken death, just learn from them and make the changes needed to bring dead things back to life once again. We have all struggled with this lesson.

Toby Mac wrote the lyrics to "*Speak Life*." What an amazing song! I would encourage you to go on YouTube and listen to it. Then start speaking life, hope, and love through the darkest night and watch as His hope starts rising up in your spirit.

Use your words to inspire . . . life!

11

Don't Bow to Satan's Bullying!

"All this I will give you," he said, "if you will bow down and worship me" (Matthew 4:9).

Although Jesus never bowed to the evil tactics of the Devil, believe it or not, many Christians—even strong, Spirit-filled Christians—bow to something evil every day without realizing it. When the heat of the battle became fierce, admittedly, I did too! And what was this evil I bowed to? I began to consciously pull back from what God had called and anointed me to do, in hopes that the enemy would back off too. But guess what? All that did was grieve the heart of God and encourage the enemy all the more.

Oh, he was loving it, all right. And why wouldn't he? Now, because I had withdrawn from the frontlines, he was in control of the battle once again. Yes, without realizing it, I was bowing to the enemy of my soul and giving him control, not only over me, but over my battlefield too. I had inadvertently begun to cower to him, thus making my adversary feel even more empowered. Without realizing it, I had given him what he wanted all along—my white flag of surrender!

Looking back now, from a spiritual perspective, it's easy to understand what was going on. In essence, the enemy had conquered one of God's earthly ground forces, and now that I was powerless and cowering in fear, he was off and running again. With me out of the fight, it was easier than ever before for him to destroy my young son's life. His merciless beatings accelerated to a whole new level of cruelty on my already beaten down spirit. Oh yes, he was even more confident that his evil battle plans would be triumphant. Inadvertently, I had empowered him all the more to press in and finish us off.

You see, it wasn't that I had stopped fighting and praying for my son and his victory over the evil one. Oh no; that was a war I was willing to fight until my dying breath if necessary. But I had backed off from doing what God called me to do for the lost. What I didn't realize at the time was that my call to see the lost saved was also what empowered me for the fight. When I backed off in this area, in hopes that the constant incoming attacks would die down, I didn't realize how much strength and hope I'd received every time I won the lost to Christ. You see, leading the lost to Christ brought me great joy, and joy brings strength. *Do not grieve, for the joy of the LORD is your strength.* (Nehemiah 8:10) Not only that, the enemy took it as a sign that I was pulling back from the fight all together, therefore, he pressed in all the more for the final kill while I was weak!

May we never forget that we were called to this fight! And what are we fighting for? All that God treasures most in this world . . . people. And what frontline should we start fighting on first? Our families. If we lose those closest to us, then we have lost the very ones God gave us to nurture and protect. Yes, we must draw a line in the sand right there first. But that doesn't mean we stop trying to conquer the rest of the world for Christ's sake too.

Can you relate to my story? Are you bowing to something today and grieving the heart of God too? Are you weary in the battle and ready to back down from what God has anointed you to do? If so, then let the story of my weakness give you the strength to press on in the fight and keep doing what you were called to do. Don't let the weariness define you or keep you back from what you're supposed to be doing for the kingdom of God. That's what empowers us in the first place. If we give up there, then we have retreated and fallen back from our original purpose, call and destiny. Just because our kids have been taken captive doesn't mean we allow the enemy to take our destiny and purpose captive too.

Whatever you were doing for the kingdom's sake before you went under attack, is still what you're called to while under attack. Trust me, that's why Satan hates us to begin with. We are "difference makers" in the kingdom and he hates us for it. Let's face it: If we weren't a threat and making a difference in people's lives, then why bother with us?

Our call is what makes us powerful in the kingdom of God. The more we operate in our call, the stronger we get. When we back down in this area, we become complacent and weak. Only God knows how often our pastors are under intense pressure from the enemy in their personal lives, for all the good they do in our lives. And I'm sure they sometimes want to give up and wave their white flag of surrender too. Nonetheless, their call and purpose for shepherding us and the desire to save the lost keeps them pushing on through in the fight. I'm so thankful that my many pastors over the years didn't give up on their call to minister to me.

But you see, according to the Word of God, we are all ministers of God:

And you will be called priest of the LORD, you will be named ministers of our God (Isaiah 61:6).

From the day you were saved, you became a minister of God to those around you, and that includes the lost and dying world. You were made to make a difference in the lives of others. You were saved to minister to others. Think about it: when you share your testimony and give praise to God for all that He has done in your life, how does that make you feel? Good, right? It's what empowers you and compels you to overcome. Again, how did they overcome the enemy?

And they overcame him by the blood of the Lamb, and by the word of their testimony; and they loved not their lives unto the death (Revelation 12:11 KJV).

So keep on sharing your testimony and ministering to those around you, overcomers. That's when your spiritual, overcoming strength starts rising up on the inside of you. It's the very thing that empowers us against the enemy and enables us to overtake him when we're in the fight. Don't ever stop doing what God has called you to do as a minister of God, then you will be more than a conqueror on the battlefield, where God has called you to fight for those on the frontlines . . . your family!

***

Are you bowing to worry? Remember, worry is brought on by fear, so be careful—if you allow this to continue you will soon become a "noble worrier" instead of what God called you to be: a noble *mighty* warrior.

Don't beat yourself up too badly if you find yourself giving in to worry; just turn it around and let it be the lightning bolt that reminds you to pray. That's what I used it for—a trigger to pray! The truth is, if you have time to worry, you have time to pray. I believe that's why Paul told us to pray without ceasing. If we can worry without ceasing, then we can pray without ceasing too.

Especially during difficult times, Satan will plant worrisome thoughts in your mind to torment you. As I said before, be very careful what you focus on, because you can make room for him to come in and take over—don't bow to it! Don't empower that worrisome thought by giving it your focus. Again, what you focus on you empower, so replace those thoughts immediately with the Word of God and His promises.

I'll never forget the day when I was deep into worry about my son, and suddenly I heard the Lord interrupt my worrisome thoughts and say, *You are worrying.* I responded back by saying right out loud, "I am."

So busted!

It may sound noble to say we are so worried about someone or something, however, to the Lord we are showing Him that we don't trust Him to take care of the matter, especially if we've already taken it to

Him in prayer.

Perhaps, you've found yourself bowing to feelings or thoughts of doubt, fear, or even depression. All of these are the evil one's weapons of warfare straight out of the pit of *hell*! Simply and immediately tell Satan, "I WON'T BOW TO YOUR THOUGHTS, SATAN! I take that thought captive in Jesus' name!" Just turn it around on that old Devil. Take captive what took you captive and tell it to become obedient to what God has to say about the matter! Take authority over it; you have the authority and power because the Holy Spirit of God lives inside of you. Take captive your captives instead. I know I've discussed this in previous chapters, but this is so important and powerful, it just can't be stressed enough.

Did you know this even works in our dreams? It sure does! I've put it to the test many times. Sometimes, in a dream, the only word I could get out was "*Jesus!*" In a nightmare, I would often times find myself in a paralyzed state due to the presence of so much evil, but if I could manage to speak His name, I was immediately released by the evil spirit! I'm telling you, this stuff works!

We demolish arguments and every pretension that sets itself up against the knowledge of God, and we take captive every thought to make it obedient to Christ (2 Corinthians 10:5).

I love the thought of demolishing Satan's arguments and taking him captive instead of him taking me captive. I learned to use this method of fighting back continually during my dark days, and I still use it to this day when I catch myself worrying. I know it's rude to interrupt someone when they are talking to you, but I get a real charge out of interrupting that old Devil and telling him to *shut up*! Then I immediately speak faith filled words: "Old Devil, hear the word of the LORD! The Lord says this child is *His* child, and those dry bones are coming to life, and when they do, he will overcome you and defeat your evil plans by the power of his testimony and the blood of the Lamb." Just put that old Devil on notice that his days are numbered!

Have you ever noticed how people who don't want to hear the truth or talk about God will leave your presence as quickly as possible when you give your testimony? Well, it's pretty much the same way with the old demons. Trust me; it works every time!

Paul tells us in 2 Corinthians 10:4, we use *spiritual* weapons to defeat the Devil. As I said before, you are in a spiritual battle, therefore you need to use God's Word with all the power and the authority He has given you, in order to defeat this enemy. Keep in mind, he's just as determined as you are to win this battle, so reach into your belt of truth and take out God's supernatural weapons, which carry divine power and demolish the Devil's strongholds, even before they have time to be built up in your mind.

They have divine power to demolish strongholds (2 Corinthians 10:4).

Are you having a hard time right now with finances? Are you worried that you could possibly lose everything? Don't bow to that thought—God is your provider. Every time you are tempted to worry, tell the Lord, *I trust You Lord!* Say it with all your heart, as though everything depends on Him coming through for you. By doing this, you are putting up your spiritual shield of faith and extinguishing those fiery darts of the evil one. This is truly faith in action, and it pleases the Lord. I can't tell you how many countless times I have said those very words with the utmost confidence that God would come through for me. No matter what I was tempted to worry about, I would put up my shield of faith against those worrisome thoughts and let the Lord know I was counting on Him.

And without faith it is impossible to please God (Hebrews 11:6).

Prayer and faith work hand in hand to move the hands of God to act on our behalf as we pray to Him. Yes, as believers, we have fellowship with God the Father through the Holy Spirit. Therefore when we pray, Paul says we have the ability *to move the hands of God by prayer* (1 Corinthians 2:16 TLB).

So every time you notice you've been taken captive to worry, prayerfully say, "I trust you, Lord!" Then visualize the hands of God moving in to stop the evil ones from tormenting you. Sometimes I would say it right out loud, as my personal declaration of faith. Not only to let the enemy know who I was trusting in, but to deflect his fiery arrows before they got a firm grip on my mind. Doing this helped me reset my mind on the things above and regain my spiritual focus. Yes, I would say or pray those words of faith as if the Lord was right there listening to me, because He was!

Jesus knows our thoughts, but the Devil doesn't. He just reacts according to the way we are acting and the things we are saying. Don't draw him in with your words! Again, like any bully, he's just trying to get a rise out of you.

Jesus knew their thoughts and said to them, "Every kingdom divided against itself will be ruined, and every city or household divided against itself will not stand" (Matthew 12:25).

It's time to divide up those demonic kingdom thoughts with words of faith that declare which side we are on. Since he can't read our thoughts as God can, we need to make sure he knows what's on our minds by saying and praying words of faith right out loud. Say, "I will stand undivided with Christ, and I won't bow to you, Satan, or your worrisome thoughts!" If doing this isn't convenient at the time, then say it with your actions.

I'm reminded once again of the three young Hebrew men in the Bible who stood together in their undivided devotion to God and refused to bow down and worship the king's idol. So be tenacious and hold on to what you believe, just like those young warriors did. Don't you bow down either and lose your reward. Not one of them backed down from the confident trust they had in their God, and not one of them lost their blessing either, even though they didn't do it for the blessing. At that point in their overwhelming emotional battle, they were determined to show their uncompromising devotion to the Lord their God.

Nevertheless, it was only after they stood their ground with the evil king and went through with their words of faith into the fiery furnace that they received their reward.

Think about it: they didn't realize in that terrifying moment that God was already there just waiting to reward them for their courage and honor in the face of a horrifying death. God's Word tells us that He is a rewarder of those who earnestly seek him, so keep on doing what is right in the eyes of God, my friend.

And without faith it is impossible to please God, because anyone who comes to him must believe that he exists and that he rewards those who earnestly seek him. (Hebrews 11:6).

In short, they were ready to be thrown into a literal burning furnace filled with hot coals of fire before they would bow down and worship another god. (Read Deuteronomy 32:16-20 for more information about other gods.)

I know I shared some of this story before in an earlier chapter, however it's so relevant to the message God has given me in this chapter that I want to share parts of it with you again in greater detail.

Afterward, when the king got up to look in the furnace, he couldn't believe his eyes, so he asked his advisers, *"Weren't there three men that we tied up and threw into the fire?"* They replied, *"Certainly, Your Majesty."* He said, *"Look! I see four men walking around in the fire, unbound and unharmed, and the fourth looks like a son of the gods."* *Nebuchadnezzar then approached the opening of the blazing furnace and shouted, "Shadrach, Meshach and Abednego, servants of the Most High God, come out! Come here!"* (Daniel 3:24-26).

Again, what an amazing story of courage and devotion to the true and living God in the face of a horrible death! When your faith is as strong as that of these three Hebrew men in this story, the watching world can't help but acknowledge who your God is! Think about it: you are a servant of the *same* Most High God!

Many believe the fourth man was Jesus Christ, and that's what I believe too. He is our faithful friend and rescuer; the true and living God who's more than willing to walk through the fire with us. Also, notice that we didn't see the fourth man until the boys were already in the fire. Nevertheless, don't you know He was already there, helping them to be strong and courageous? I can testify from the many times I felt like I was about to be thrown into the fiery furnace, God was right there giving me the courage and strength I needed to face my fiery trial.

Deuteronomy 31:6 says, *Be strong and courageous. Do not be afraid or terrified because of them, for the LORD your God goes with you; he will never leave you nor forsake you.* That means He is always with us, we just need to stand firm in our faith as they did, proving that we believe He's right there with us as we stand our ground. The story goes on to say that when the men came out of the fire, *they saw that the fire had not harmed their bodies, nor was a hair of their heads singed; their robes were not scorched, and there was no smell of fire on them* (Daniel 3:27).

If you will refuse to bow to the Devil and remain devoted to the Lord Jesus, no matter what the cost, even unto death, He will rescue you too from whatever fiery furnace the enemy of your soul tries to throw you and your family into. I believe the same fiery trial the enemy tried to use to destroy you and your loved one will soon become a holy consuming fire within you!

For our "God is a consuming fire" (Hebrews 12:29).

Not only that, you won't even look or smell like you've ever *been* in a fire.

I'll never forget the day when the war was finally over that I had the privilege of meeting a true prophetess of the Lord, who knew nothing about my past. She looked at me and said, "Charlotte, I can't see anything but peace when I look at you. You wear it like royalty." That's when I knew for sure that the fiery furnace hadn't disfigured me, but God had used it to transfigure me to reflect His Son's peace. Yes, the Prince of Peace was shining through me. Although I couldn't see it as she did, I certainly could feel it.

Peace I leave with you; my peace I give you (John 14:27).

Even though I now walk in an incredible peace that He has given me, I still remember those feelings of being overwhelmed as the enemy ganged up on me with one crisis after another. Some days, it felt as if he was turning up the heat in my already unbearable fiery furnace. But, my friend, it's during our most horrendous times that we must stand firm in our faith, just like those young men did . . . even if the furnace gets turned up seven times hotter! Yes, we too must take on the same warrior attitude and say, as they did, *Our God is able, but even if he does not deliver us, we won't bow to you Satan!*

Perhaps your pain is too paralyzing for you to move right now, like mine was some days. Then stand, soldier! Stand with your boots firmly planted on the Word of God.

After you have done everything . . . stand (Ephesians 6:13).

Don't let the pain of that moment force you to give up—rise up and don't bow to it! Don't let it define who you are, because you already know whose you are. That's when the true worshipers stand tall and cry out in faith saying, *We do not know what to do, but our eyes are on you Lord* (2 Chronicles 20:12). As I said before, don't even try to figure it all out. Just *trust in the Lord with all your heart and lean not on your own understanding* (Proverbs 3:5).

I believe God sometimes allows us to go through difficult times of testing in order for us to see where we are in our devotion to Him. Peter certainly discovered where his devotion to Christ was when he heard the cock crow after denying Christ three times in one night. That's why it's so important that you stop bowing to the fearful lies of the enemy and trust the Lord your God with all your heart. Pass the test and watch how quickly God promotes and rewards you. At the end of Peter's life, he was not only ready to die for Christ name's sake, tradition has it, he didn't feel worthy to even be crucified in the same manner as Christ. Therefore, he requested to be crucified upside down.

So rebuke the Devil, don't bow to the evil thoughts he puts in your head. Take back your mind and you will take back your joy-filled, God-given life again.

The Word of God says, *For you died, and your life is now hidden with Christ in God* (Colossians 3:3). Yes, we came into this world to die, but not just a physical death at the end of our lives. Oh no, it was to die to ourselves, and what we had planned while here on this earth. Paul said, *I have been crucified with Christ and I no longer live, but Christ lives in me. The life I now live in the body, I live by faith in the Son of God, who loved me and gave himself for me* (Galatians 2:20).

If the old you has died, then it's time to find that new life God has hidden in Christ for you. If you want to find the fullness of this new life, then it may be time to go deeper with Him in your personal walk. If God is drawing you out of your comfort zone and into the deep waters right now, then it just could be to die. Remember when I said at the beginning of this book that God was preparing me to die? Well, now you know what I meant. The question is, are you willing to go into the deepest, darkest valley to find what God has hidden for you in your new life with Christ and let everything you dreamed of die? Because it's when you willfully allow yourself to be led by the Spirit of God into the unknown wilderness that the transfiguration process begins and the old you starts to die. Therefore, I can't encourage you enough to allow Him to lead you by His Spirit into whatever wilderness is necessary in order for you to find your new life in Him. Don't give up until you find the inexpressible treasures that can only be found in this hidden life with Christ. *For as many as are led by the Spirit of God, they are the sons of God* (Romans 8:14 KJV).

Who are you allowing to lead you right now? Is Satan leading you with his fearful thoughts? Are you making serious decisions out of fear? If so, take a stand right now and begin to let God guide your thoughts.

May we never forget that Jesus was led into the wilderness by the Spirit of God, and that same Spirit won't shield you from the requirements of "a son of God." Keep in mind, Satan wants the same thing from you that he wanted from Jesus during his wilderness time of testing—to bow down and worship him.

"All this I will give you," he said, *"if you will bow down and worship me"* (Matthew 4:9).

Now, let's take a moment and think about the spiritual high Jesus must have been on right before He was led into the demonic wilderness. He had just heard His Father's words of admiration: *This is my Son, whom I love; with him I am well pleased* (Matthew 3:17). And right before that thrilling moment, the Bible says, *as soon as Jesus was baptized, he went up out of the water. At that moment heaven was opened, and he saw the Spirit of God descending like a dove and alighting on him* (Matthew 3:16). The next thing we read, Jesus is being led by the Spirit of God into the wilderness valley where Satan is waiting there to test His devotion to the Father. Trust me, this was a demonic battlefield, one where the Son of God would prove to Satan *whose He was*, and there was no way Jesus Christ was going to bow down to Satan and surrender His God-given identity! He overcame the lies and testing of Satan because He knew not only *whose* He was, but *who* He was . . . the Son of the true and living God.

Simon Peter answered, "You are the Messiah, the Son of the living God." (Matthew 16:16).

My friend, that's why it's so important that we know whose we are and who we are . . . sons and daughters of God. Because if we have this knowledge hidden deep within our hearts, we have truly found the life that was hidden in Christ, and we too will walk in the same power and authority that Jesus did!

Very truly I tell you, whoever believes in me will do the works I have been doing, and they will do even greater things than these (John 14:12).

Although my wilderness valley and time of testing, in no way compares to what Jesus went through for us, I can see some parallels here from my vision and my own journey through the wilderness. The truth is, He's been where we are at right now, and He knows His way through this demon-filled wilderness valley too. Also, He wants to journey with us during this difficult time, so that He can help lead us safely through until we reach the other side.

Jesus' story reminds me of what happened to me right before I went into my demonic wilderness and valley of testing. First, Jesus affirmed His great love for me. Then He led me by the hand into the wilderness valley below, where I too would be tested by the Devil. Although God loved me dearly, He did not shield me from the requirements that were placed on me as a child of God. And if He's bringing you into this deeper walk with Him, He won't shield you either.

My friend, you must *know* who you are—a *royal* child of the only true and living God, the eternal King!

But the Lord is the true God; he is the living God, the eternal King (Jeremiah 10:10).

So stand firm in your faith, knowing who you are in Christ, then you will be able to withstand whatever Satan has prepared for you in the deep, dark wilderness valley. Unshakable faith in God is what gives you the power and strength to stand in the day of battle. I've said it before and it's worth saying again: Satan already knows who you are and the power and authority you possess: he's just testing you to see if you know it too!

And God raised us up with Christ and seated us with him in the heavenly realms in Christ Jesus (Ephesians 2:6).

Let's face it. Satan already knew who Christ was, he was just testing Him to see if *He* knew who He was. It's the same old trick he plays on us when we're in our own wilderness. I can't stress this enough, because you've got to get this concept. If we are seated with Him in heavenly realms (which means spiritual realms), then we must understand that our set place while here on earth is with Him, right now, in the spiritual realm. And if our set place is with Him, then we rule and reign with Him from His seat of power and authority. Yes, Christ has given us all authority and power, therefore we now operate with Him in the heavenly realm as His royal children. Remember, 1 Peter 2:9 says: *But you are a chosen people, a royal priesthood . . . God's special possession, that you may declare the praises of him who called you out of the darkness into his wonderful light.* Jesus said, *I have given you authority to trample on snakes and scorpions and to overcome all the power of the enemy; nothing will harm you* (Luke 10:19).

Spiritually speaking, we are already there with Him, ruling and reigning over the enemy as God's special possessions, and trampling him under our feet. You might say we are God's secret weapon against the evil one! We need to get a vision of this operation center in our minds as we operate from that place of honor, authority, and power as children of the Most High God. We need to put the Devil on notice and let him know that we are well aware of who we are, and the power we possess *because* of whose we are in Christ.

In other words, we are living in a human world, but we are having a spiritual experience. Keep in mind, we are only on a pilgrimage, just passing through . . . this is NOT our home!

Unfortunately, many Christians either don't understand this concept or have lost sight of this heavenly perspective; as a result, they have lost out on knowing who they really are as well as their God given power and authority. Sadly, many of them will die in the wilderness valley and forfeit their reward of the Promised Land that God had prepared for them. That doesn't mean that they're not going to heaven, only that they were *destroyed from lack of knowledge* while still in the wilderness. (Hosea 4:6)

We don't have to put up with the rulers of darkness and all the scare tactics they try to use on us. They are bullies who enjoy terrorizing people, and, believe me, like any bully, they will keep on tormenting you until they get what they want . . . you to bow (or cower) to them.

As most people already know, if you let a bully keep bullying you, the bullying only gets worse. Why? Because they feel more empowered every time you cower to them. Oh, and what happens if you start to get up and fight back after a bully thinks he has power over you? He becomes even more indignant and starts turning up his old taunts, telling you what a loser you are. Sound familiar?

Goliath stood and shouted a taunt across to the Israelites. "Why are you all coming out to fight?" he called. "I am the Philistine champion, but you are only the servants of Saul (1 Samuel 17:8 NLT).

Is this what the bully of your soul is shouting to you right now? Is he yelling out his usual taunts and reminding you of all the times you bowed down and cowered to him in fear, and asking you why you're bothering to stand your ground now? Is he comparing his size and armor to yours and trying to intimidate you into backing down once again? Then you have just encountered the same bully the Israelites did on that day.

Although this giant's name was Goliath, that wasn't actually his real name, or, might we say, his real spirit name. Satan, the giant of all bullies, was shouting those taunts at God's people that day. Yes, the old ancient giant of old was challenging the people of God and they were cowering and shaking with fear at the sight of him:

Choose one man to come down here and fight me! If he kills me, then we will be your slaves. But if I kill him, you will be our slaves! I defy the armies of Israel today! Send me a man who will fight me!" When Saul and the Israelites heard this, they were terrified and deeply shaken. (1 Samuel 17:8-11 NLT).

Then, one person rose up and took the Devil's challenge. His name was David, a young boy the Bible tells us. Nevertheless, this boy knew *whose* he was and who he was in God—a son of the living God.

When David arrived at the battlefield that day, he was appalled by what he heard and saw happening:

He arrived at the camp just as the Israelite army was leaving for the battlefield with shouts and battle cries. Soon the Israelite and Philistine forces stood facing each other, army against army. David left his things with the keeper of supplies and hurried out to the ranks to greet his brothers. As he was talking with them, Goliath, the Philistine champion from Gath, came out from the Philistine ranks. Then David heard him shout his usual taunt to the army of Israel. As soon as the Israelite army saw him, they began to run away in fright (1 Samuel 17:20-24 NLT).

And this is what David said: *Who is this pagan Philistine anyway, that he is allowed to defy the armies of the living God?* (1 Samuel 17:26 NLT). In other words, "Who does he think he is, talking to the warriors of God like that?"

We need to ask ourselves the same question when the enemy starts his usual old taunts in our ears. I guess the Israelites had become desensitized from hearing those same old taunts and forgot whose they were because, according to the Word of God, all of them ran in fright.

Can you imagine how disappointed God was every time this happened? He was right there, ready to fight with them, but no one would go out and face this demon giant with Him. So it seems as though He just waited for the right person to come along who would get in the fight. Oh yes, God could have defeated him in a second, but He wanted His warriors to get in the fight with Him, and, until they did, He was willing to wait on them to make the first move. Is God waiting for you to make the first move too?

Think about it: when David arrived, *they were leaving for the battlefield with shouts and battle cries.* It sounds to me like they were all talk and no fight. How foolish they must have looked to the enemy. No wonder Goliath thought he could taunt and bully them. Oh, but when the one arrived who wasn't all talk, but was ready to actively get in the fight, things started to change quickly. Nonetheless, not without some more taunts from the evil one:

Goliath walked out toward David with his shield bearer ahead of him, sneering in contempt at this ruddy-faced boy. "Am I a dog," he roared at David, "that you come at me with a stick?" And he cursed David by the names of his gods. "Come over here, and I'll give your flesh to the birds and wild animals!" Goliath yelled (1 Samuel 17:41-44 NLT).

But David, didn't let those old taunts bother him. Oh no! He came back with some faith-filled words for that old demon:

You come to me with sword, spear, and javelin, but I come to you in the name of the LORD of Heaven's Armies—the God of the armies of Israel, whom you have defied. Today the LORD will conquer you, and I will kill you and cut off your head. And then I will give the dead bodies of your men to the birds and wild animals, and the whole world will know that there is a God in Israel! And everyone assembled here will know that the LORD rescues his people, but not with sword and spear. This is the LORD's battle, and he will give you to us!" (1 Samuel 17:45-47 NLT).

Now those are some faith-filled words! And who was he counting on to be in the fight with him that day? David said it: *Today the Lord will conquer you.* We must do the same thing in our lives. Tell the old ancient giant that the Lord will conquer him this day, then go on to tell him what you're going to do to him that will bring glory to God. After you say those words of faith, actively move in the giant's direction by doing whatever the Lord tells you to do. If God asks you to fast and pray, then ask Him what kind of fast He wants from you. When the disciples were up against a powerful demon, they asked Jesus, *"Why could we not cast it out?" So He said to them, "This kind can come out by nothing but prayer and fasting"* (Mark 9:28-29 NKJV). That tells me that we receive more power to defeat the evil one when we combine fasting and prayer together. Do whatever the Spirit encourages you to do. If He asks you to sing your victory song by faith, then sing songs with victory written all over them. What if He tells you to give a shout of praise and declare what He is going to do by prophesying? No matter what the Lord instructs you to do, just start doing it by faith, believing that He is in the fight with you and that what you are declaring will come to pass!

God is the same God today as He was back then, and He still wants to be in the fight with us. Not only that, the old ancient giant is still out there, taunting God's people, even today, and causing fear to rise up. Don't give into those lies and taunts any longer by cowering down and running away. You are who the Word of God says you are. Therefore, say to that old bully Satan, *"Who is this Devil anyway, that he is allowed to defy the armies of the living God? You are a liar, and I will conquer and defeat you today, because I am already more than you will ever be in Christ Jesus!"*

In all these things we are more than conquerors through him who loved us (Romans 8:37).

Paul goes on in Romans to say, *For I am convinced that neither death nor life, neither angels nor demons, neither the present nor the future, nor any powers, neither height nor depth, nor anything else in all creation, will be able to separate us from the love of God that is in Christ Jesus our Lord* (Romans 8:38-39).

Absolutely nothing can defeat or separate you from the God who walks by your side!

I keep my eyes always on the LORD. With him at my right hand, I will not be shaken (Psalm 16:8).

As you can see from reading the story in 1 Samuel, it's time to rise up and join in the fight. Say to the enemy, *This is the LORD's battle, and he will give you to us!* (1 Samuel 17:45-47 NLT).

If you keep running, Satan will take everything you have, including your marriage and your *entire* family. You must stand your ground with him. As believers, we should never allow fearful thoughts or scary situations that we know are from the evil one to influence our decisions in a negative way. If we do, then we are allowing ourselves to be led by his evil spirit and not God's Holy Spirit. Again I say, *for God hath not given us the spirit of fear; but of power, and of love, and of a sound mind* (2 Timothy 1:7 KJV).

When I read this story, the Lord encouraged me to take back the sound mind He had given me and get back in the fight! So, my friend, I want to encourage you to do the same thing. Take up your shield of faith and deflect those fiery darts of fear too. Use your spiritual armor—that's why God gave it to you. God is requiring you to do your part too in this battle, and that means you need to rise up and armor up, so you'll be ready to fight back when the Devil strikes with his evil spirit of fear! Again, you do this by remembering whose you are and your set place of authority—you're the one in charge when the Devil shows up, not him! This is your command post and operation center—not his! Take your instruction from the Word of God and operate from God's vantage point on high . . . in heavenly places. I'm sure God has a much better view from up there to see what the enemy is up to. Jesus said, *Very truly I tell you, the Son can do nothing by himself; he can only do what he sees his Father doing, because whatever the Father does the Son also does.* (John 5:19) Jesus not only kept His eyes fixed on the Father, He operated from His set place of authority on high in the heavenly realms.

I will instruct you and teach you in the way you should go; I will counsel you with my loving eye on you. Do not be like the horse or the mule, which have no understanding but must be controlled by bit and bridle or they will not come to you (Psalm 32:8-9).

Again, every morning, get up, get dressed, and put on your spiritual armor. Don't be lazy. Get up early if you have to. Get dressed and ready for the battle. Because you know the old bully is sure to be hiding in the darkness somewhere, just waiting to jump you. It's time to *fight the good fight of the faith* in the heavenly realms. (1 Timothy 6:12).

I love to visualize myself putting on my armor as I take up my shield of faith and the sword of His Spirit, the Word of God. To this day, I do this every morning while in prayer. It makes me feel like an invincible warrior of God . . . Watch out, Devil!

Always be mindful that these are your God-given, divine spiritual weapons of warfare; it's your protection on the battlefield. Trust me: in the heavenly realms, they have open carry—it's okay to openly display your weapons for all to see. Wear them daily and let the enemy know you are packing the power of God, and you won't back down or bow down to him no matter what he comes against you with today!

Did you know that the shields used in battle during biblical times covered the entire front of a soldier's body as he crouched behind it for protection? That's right! But there was no shield or armor for his backside if he ran the other way and went AWOL! Therefore be determined to keep your guard up, spiritually speaking, and stand your ground by guarding your mind with the helmet of salvation firmly in place and your shield of faith up at all times! Speak His Word—it's your defensive sword—and stay in the fight!

Keep your spiritual fervor and never lose your spiritual edge when using your armor—that armor puts Satan on notice when he sees you coming. And trust me, he can't help but see you coming, as your armor of light pierces the darkness. ...*put on the armor of light.* (Romans 13:12)

Immediately, he recognizes that you are a well-trained and highly qualified warrior of God. A force to be reckoned with! I can guarantee in that moment, not only will the enemy flee, but all of hell will know whose you are—one of His glorious ones who won't back down or bow down to their evil tactics. When you're able to do this on a consistent basis, you too will start to realize the spiritual power and authority God has given you. Suddenly you will have a new awareness of who you really are—a true and fearless warrior, a warrior of the living God, one who's highly approved by God, just as Jesus was.

Again I say, don't be led by the spirit of the Devil into a place of defeat. Don't surrender your mind to his thoughts; only be led by the Spirit of God and live in the place of certain victory. Fight from that vantage point and be determined to walk in the light *as He is in the light*

(1 John 1:7). You are wearing His armor of light, my friend, go and pierce the darkness!

The night is nearly over; the day is almost here. So let us put aside the deeds of darkness and put on the armor of light (Romans 13:12).

When you see yourself rising up with this kind of steadfast resolve and power, know that the dark valley days are nearly over and glorious ones are just up ahead. This will be your sign and your finest hour! Oh yeah, it's almost time to sing a new song of praise to the Lord your God, because He is doing a new thing in your heart and in your circumstances. Yes, when you get to this overcoming point in your journey, that long dark night in the valley is almost over. This old dark journey through the wilderness valley will soon be a song of praise in your heart for the wonderful faithfulness of your God.

Rejoice in the Lord always. I will say it again: Rejoice! (Philippians 4:4).

Paul understood that his circumstances didn't dictate his faith level. He had spiritual eyes that could see through the darkness, because he had learned how to walk by faith in the light of Jesus' glory. Again I say, rejoice in the victory, as though you already have it, especially while you're in the darkest demon valley. Oh yes, God is doing a new thing inside of you while you're in this wilderness valley, and no one will be more amazed than you. That's why the Lord says, *Forget the former things; do not dwell on the past. See, I am doing a new thing!* (Isaiah 43:18-19). Don't let darkness overtake you, *but overcome evil with good* (Romans 12:21).

Hate what is evil; cling to what is good . . . Never be lacking in zeal, but keep your spiritual fervor, serving the Lord (Romans 12:9-11).

Satan is always trying to destroy our zeal for what God has called us to do. He knows if we are filled with God's zeal and spiritual fervor, we are unstoppable! Don't let him cut in on you and keep you back from running your race and obtaining your prize. God has something hidden for you, and you'll only find it as you run your race. Keep your relationship with Christ first place in your life, that way you're sure to come in first place when you reach the finish line. Don't let the enemy discourage you either; you're running a good race now, my friend. Don't let him cut in on you anymore!

The Lord will march out like a champion, like a warrior he will stir up his zeal; with a shout he will raise the battle cry and will triumph over his enemies (Isaiah 42:13).

Every time you feel discouraged and defeated, stir up your zeal by harkening back to your mountaintop experiences with God. Encourage yourself in the Lord and refresh your mind once again on your triumphant LORD, and hear what He has to say about you, mighty warrior. Let those memories of past battles you've won with God on your side give you the courage needed to press on in the race He has set before you. Let them remind you of who you are in Him and how faithful God has always been to you in every battle. That's what David did when the Devil spoke through King Saul, trying to convince him that he was too young and small to defeat the giant:

"Don't be ridiculous!" Saul replied. "There's no way you can fight this Philistine and possibly win! You're only a boy, and he's been a man of war since his youth." But David persisted. "I have been taking care of my father's sheep and goats," he said. "When a lion or a bear comes to steal a lamb from the flock, I go after it with a club and rescue the lamb from its mouth. If the animal turns on me, I catch it by the jaw and club it to death. I have done this to both lions and bears, and I'll do it to this pagan Philistine, too, for he has defied the armies of the living God! The LORD who rescued me from the claws of the lion and the bear will rescue me from this Philistine!" (1 Samuel 17:33-37).

He is our rescuer, and He will rescue you again and again, my friend! David understood the power of speaking those things that were not as though they were. He spoke his victory into being, with confident faith that God would never let him down. He knew if he did his part, God would show up and do His. We can all take notes from this young warrior of God.

Later on in the book of 1 Samuel, we see the mighty warrior King David, returning from battle with his men, only to find their town destroyed by fire and their wives, sons, and daughters taken captive. But what did King David do? *David encouraged himself in the Lord his God* (1 Samuel 30:6 KJV). You see, not only had the enemy taken everything precious to David, but the very men he had once trusted with his life were talking about killing him.

I'm sure there was much backbiting going on at that moment of weakness in their hurting lives. And I'm also sure it grieved David's heart to know the ones he trusted most would turn on him in such a vicious way. But David didn't let himself get bogged down in the weakness of those around him, nor did he let the murderous threats make him lose focus. Oh no, this man of God stayed in his set place and sought the Lord with his whole heart for wisdom and understanding in what to do. The Word of God says, *and David inquired of the LORD, "Shall I pursue this raiding party? Will I overtake them?" "Pursue them," he answered. "You will certainly overtake them and succeed in the rescue"* (1 Samuel 30:8). And that's what we must do too when the enemy comes and takes our family members captive . . . inquire of the Lord! After He gives us a clear answer and a battle plan, then we are ready to go after our enemy and overtake him . . . we will succeed in the rescue!

And that's exactly what God is doing right now with our families. As we inquire of Him, He begins to instruct us on how to proceed in a way that takes our emotions out of the equation and puts His plans and strategies in place, so we can succeed in our rescue attempt too.

Trust me, when you win this battle and bring your child or loved one back home, you will be like King David and his men . . . singing a new song! Oh yes, a new song of praise and thanksgiving to the Lord your God for all His wonderful deeds and goodness toward you during what was once an extremely difficult time in your life. Victory is sweet, my friend, and the battle is worth it!

I will tell of the LORD'S unfailing love. I will praise the LORD for all he has done. I will rejoice in his great goodness (Isaiah 63:7 NLT).

12

The Battle Belongs to the Lord

*But the eyes of the LORD are on those who fear him, on those
whose hope is in his unfailing love, to deliver them from death*
(Psalm 33:18-19).

One day, while I reflected on my many years of fighting what seemed like one raging battle after another, I was awed by the thought of how the Lord had faithfully fought each battle right by my side. I thought about the perfect battle instructions He had given me for every battle, and how His strategic plan led me from one amazing victory to another. Without a doubt, by now He had proven Himself faithful over the years and I knew I could trust Him completely.

It was during this same time that the Lord's hand was very heavy on me to surrender everything I held most precious in this life completely over to Him. Although, I have shared portions of this story about the day I surrendered my will for my son's life to God's will in previous chapters, I want you to know, it didn't happen overnight. Oh no, I'd tried many times throughout the years to lay my oldest son down on God's altar, but I would always go back and pick him up again. The truth is, I never fully surrendered him to the Lord, let alone my other two children and everything else I dearly cherished.

It's important that you understand where I was in my spiritual walk with the Lord at this point in the journey. I'm going to refer to a teaching by John Paul Jackson that I heard a few years after I came to this place of complete surrender. Nevertheless, it perfectly described my entire journey and the place I was spiritually, at that very moment. He even had a name for it: *the dark hour of the spirit*. What did that mean? I have touched on this in previous chapters, but now I want to go ever deeper into what this means. It meant the time had come for me to completely surrender to the will of the Father.

In this teaching, John Paul Jackson talks about how Jesus came to that place in His own life here on earth, and all of us who are believers will eventually come to that place too. At some point, we all need to utterly surrender to the Father's will for our lives and for those we love. Why? Because it's the final step that has to be made if we want to see the powers of hell broken once and for all! With that being said, I would encourage you to not put it off, as I did, and to do it sooner than later.

Here's why: God knew the only way I would be completely free and see the glorious final victory was to do as Jesus did and surrender my will to His will. As I said before, in my heart I knew I could trust God, and I also knew it was time to lay down everything I was holding on to and trust Him explicitly. Therefore I decided that day it was time to set my mind and keep it set, and make this very important decision. With this resolve in my heart, I went before the Lord in prayer that morning, and I laid everything down on His altar, including my, now, two prodigal sons.

I poured out my heart before the Lord that day while laying down all my burdens, disappointments, doubts, fears, and my two young sons, along with my will and every treasured dream I held in my heart for them. Yes, I surrendered everything I was holding on to entirely as I laid it all down on the mercy seat of God. You might say it was a defining moment in my spiritual walk that day, and I knew from that point on there was no turning back.

After I finished relinquishing all my fears and my two earthy treasures, I made a very powerful declaration before the Lord that came from the depths of my heart as I cried out: *Though You slay me, yet will I trust in You!*

Job came to this place of surrender in his spiritual walk too, as he spoke these same words: *Though he slay me, yet will I hope in him* (Job 13:15 KJV).

From that day forward, I was totally set free from all anxiety and fear! I found myself walking in a new depth of His supernatural peace, a peace that has never left me from that day.

My peace I give you (John 14:27).

From that moment on there was no more looking back, only looking up. My eyes were fixed on Him and His perfect will for all of our lives. No longer would I teeter back and forth—like Job, my new heart's desire was the desire of His heart. It was as if I'd drawn a line in the sand that day. I made my declaration of faith right out loud, because I not only wanted the Lord to hear the cry of my heart, but I wanted to make sure all of hell heard it too. In essence, I laid it all down and told the Lord I would give Him my life, my children, and everything I cherished most in this world before I would give up on trusting in Him.

Although I never stopped hoping and believing I would live to see the final victory, I was determined to trust Him with the final results, whether I lived to see the victory or not. My heart was convinced that God would come through for me and give me the victory He promised.

When you set your mind like that, there's no more room for doubt or fear to creep in and steal your joy and peace. Oh no. My mind was set on victory no matter what the cost!

Set your minds on things above (Colossians 3:2).

There was a whole new resolve living inside of me and with that new strength came a new singlemindedness. I was determined from that day forward I was *not* going to bow down to Satan and his demons of destruction no matter how high they turned up the heat in my already fiery furnace.

I truly believe the tide of the battle turned in my favor that day. I knew in my heart that the years of anguish and tears would soon become my new song of victory!

You have seen me tossing and turning though the night. You have collected all my tears and preserved them in your bottle! You have recorded every one in your book. The very day I called for help, the tide of the battle turns. My enemies flee! (Psalm 56:8-9).

It felt as if there was a new fire blazing in my soul after that declaration, and victory was my end-all goal! To say the least, it was a day of reckoning. It was also the day God brought this scripture to life within my heart: *He has sent me to bind up the brokenhearted, to proclaim freedom for the captives and release from darkness for the prisoners, to proclaim the year of the Lord's favor and the day of vengeance of our God, to comfort all who mourn, and provide for those who grieve in Zion—to bestow on them a crown of beauty instead of ashes, the oil of joy instead of mourning, and a garment of praise instead of a spirit of despair. They will be called oaks of righteousness, a planting of the Lord for the display of his splendor* (Isaiah 61:1-3).

God's favor was upon me in a whole new way, and I knew His day of vengeance against the evil one who took my sons captive was about to be revealed.

I can honestly say, the day I laid my two Isaacs down was the day of complete surrender and freedom for my weary soul! Even so, I knew my declaration of faith would not go untested. Genesis 22:1 says, *God tested Abraham.* I would encourage you to read this entire chapter of Genesis if you're going through a time of testing too. After I finished reading this chapter, it was obvious what God was after: Abraham's *will.* God tested Abraham's devotion to Him by asking him to sacrifice the one thing he held most dear here on this earth—his promised son Isaac. The very son God had promised him a nation would be born from.

I'm sure none of this made any sense to Abraham at the time, nevertheless, he believed in his heart if he slayed his son Isaac, God would raise him back to life again. His mind was set on doing God's will and not leaning to his own understanding, therefore by faith he built his altar before the Lord. Then he laid his only son down on the altar of God and took out his knife to sacrifice him before the Lord. Although the angel of the Lord stopped Abraham right before he plunged the knife into Isaac, God saw Abraham's heart and there was no doubt he would have gone through with it, even if it meant his son's death. Without a doubt, Abraham's will was surrendered completely to God's will at all cost. Needless to say, he passed the test!

My friend, I believe with all my heart, this is the place where heaven meets earth.

Our Father in heaven, hallowed be your name, your kingdom come, your will be done, on earth as it is in heaven (Matthew 6:10).

This is where we completely let go and let God have His way. We can see clearly from Abraham's story, he was fully committed to the will of God and his mind was set. He was determined that no matter how high the cost, he would be completely obedient to God's will. Once again, God was faithful to His promise and brought forth a nation from Isaac's seed.

Often times, God will ask us to do something that makes absolutely no sense at the time, but if we will do what God tells us to do, He will be faithful to do His part too. We never know how God is going to work things out, but we can trust Him to keep His promises and bring our dead loved one back to life again.

As we read God's Word, we see where Jesus laid down His will and made that same decision in the Garden of Gethsemane:

Father, if you are willing, take this cup from me; yet not my will, but yours be done (Luke 22:42).

Yes, this is where heaven met earth as Jesus surrendered to His heavenly Father's will. His dark hour of the spirit was about to begin, as He walked out His vow before the Father.

As we look back, not only on Jesus' vow of surrender, but Abraham's surrender with his son that day on the Alter of God, we can surely agree this was a test none of us would want to be challenged with. But God says, *You shall have no other gods before me* (Exodus 20:3). God is saying to His children in this passage, anything you love more than me is an idol or god in your life. We don't think about our devotion and love for our children as being an idol, but, for me personally, my children were. You see, I could easily lay my own life down for the sake of what God wanted, but there was something more precious to me than that, and God knew I had put these two "other gods" before Him.

As I said earlier, that's why I knew it was time to lay my children on the altar of God and trust Him to completely deliver them. I knew in my heart, if they were to ever be lifted out of the valley of dry, dead bones, it was only going to be by the hand of my Almighty God.

At this point in my walk with the Lord, this was the only thing I knew for certain! Although my faith had been challenged and tested on many fronts throughout my journey, I knew this was my final test, and I would now begin to walk out my vow before the Lord and prove my pledge of surrender was authentic.

The dark hour of testing the authenticity of my vow came sooner than I expected, as I soon found myself surrounded on all sides by evil forces. Unfortunately, on this particular day, my strength was completely gone. I was so weary from all the warfare that had taken place that I had absolutely no more strength for another fight. The circumstances that surrounded my situation looked completely hopeless at that moment. Yet I was determined not to surrender. Again, I cried out to the Lord and swore my allegiance to Him, and repeated my vow once again: "Though you slay me, yet will I trust in you!"

The enemy, seeing my weariness, decided to come in for what he thought was the final blow. It was at that moment the words written in Psalm 27:17 rung out in my hea*rt: Relieve the troubles of my heart and free me from my anguish.*

It felt as though he had gathered with him several legions of evil demon forces from all the regions of the earth, and they were surrounding us on every side. There seemed to be no way out! Yes, this was the day my courageous declaration of faith would be tested! Even so, I knew my only hope was in the Lord my God and there was no turning back. The Word of God says: *Against all hope Abraham in hope believed* (Romans 4:18).

What God did next, I never saw coming. Brace yourself and pay close attention as I share this unbelievable story of hope in action.

To understand the significance of what I'm about to share with you, please turn in your Bible now and read 2 Chronicles 20 in its entirety.

This chapter was a God-breathed *now* word for me on that dreadful day. While I tried desperately to hold on to the hope I had so often found in remembering God's faithfulness in the past, as I looked at our gut-wrenching circumstances, my heart began to drown into depths of despair. Again, there seemed to be no way out. As I look at our situation, all I could see was a demon-filled valley. It was in that moment, I fell on my knees and I cried out to the Lord in utter desperation, asking for His divine intervention and guidance. I knew if God didn't intervene, there would be no hope for our situation. Like I said, it felt like Satan himself and every demon in hell had just launched a fully orchestrated attack against my family! It looked as though certain annihilation was imminent. I could feel the ominous dark clouds gathering all around as the destructive storm mounted against us. Now hold on to this picture of hopelessness while I tell you about God's divine intervention.

First, I need to give you a little background on what was going on at this time, so you'll understand why I felt so distressed and hopeless. My oldest son was still in prison and, if that wasn't already devastating enough, I was now living with and caring for my mother, who was living out her final days after being diagnosed with terminal cancer a year earlier. Oh, but that's not the worst of it! For some time, the Devil had been planning what he thought would be the perfect storm and final blow. He wasn't satisfied with trying to destroy my dreams and hopes for my oldest son. Oh no—he wanted to rip my heart out and completely finish me off by going after my youngest son too!

You must understand, the enemy won't stop or back down when you're in a war until you either surrender to him or you annihilate him completely. For me, destroying him and his evil forces was the only answer. Bowing down or backing down was out of the question at this point. So into the fiery furnace I went!

In order to understand the magnitude of this assault, I feel impressed by the Holy Spirit to share a few more details about my youngest son, that way you'll understand why Satan had him on his hit list too. I believe you'll be encouraged and filled with new hope as you see the amazing breakthrough and blessing we received by standing in faith and trusting the Lord.

My youngest son was a child I had fervently prayed for after the heartbreaking loss of my baby girl Kirsten Michelle. She died in my womb in my sixth month of pregnancy, and up until the day I lost her, I had never known such heartache. Not only had it taken me three years to conceive her, it took almost three more years for the answer to my prayers for another child to fill my aching and empty arms.

Oh, how gracious my God was when He made it up to me by giving me the most wonderful Mother's Day gift I had ever received—the gift of another baby.

Interestingly enough, the Lord had given me a special dream the first Mother's Day after losing Kirsten. In the dream, I spent the entire night playing with and nursing this same little baby. I woke up that Mother's Day morning filled with hope and joy because the dream was so real!

Three years later, at the age of thirty-seven, I became pregnant with my little dream come true. However, as the enemy would have it, this dream didn't come true without an all-out war too.

Because of losing my daughter in my sixth month of pregnancy, and with no explanation of why she died, I was continually in emotional turmoil with the fear of losing this baby too. I found myself constantly watching for any movement, just to reassure my heart that he was alive. Although I didn't say a word to anyone else in the family, it wasn't long before I realized we were all struggling with the same thoughts.

As my sixth month of pregnancy grew near, the enemy seemed to turn up the heat. My daughter, who was only thirteen years old, started having dreams that the baby died. Then I began to notice how frequently my husband asked me how I was feeling and if the baby was okay. Even my oldest son, who was only eleven years old at the time, seemed to be very concerned about each upcoming doctor's appointment. Without a doubt, Satan was using our past heartbreak to torment all of us about our new baby.

Nevertheless, the next time my daughter came to me crying about another dream where the baby died, the Lord had already shown me what to do. So, as He instructed, I took my daughter in my arms and we prayed together rebuking those tormenting oppressing demons.

Things settled down some after that, but I was still struggling with thoughts of losing him. You see, the Devil might leave for a little while when we rebuke him, but he's always waiting for his next opportunity. We see this same thing happen after Jesus rebuked Satan while being tested in the wilderness.

When the devil had finished all this tempting, he left him until an opportune time (Luke 4:13).

You see, the Devil is always looking for our times of weakness because that's his opportune time to torment us. Satan never plays fair nor gives up easily!

Not long after I prayed with my daughter, we had a divine breakthrough. One Sunday morning, as my family got ready for church, my husband and I started bickering back and forth. We pushed on through getting ready and finally we all got in the van and started off to church as usual. I was in my sixth month of pregnancy at this point and my emotions, along with my hormones, were running wild. The argument quickly escalated after we got in the van and started driving out of the neighborhood. We were only a few blocks from the house when my husband calmly pulled the van over and got out. Without a word, he began walking back home. My son quickly followed him and left me and my daughter in the van to cry alone.

Later, as I looked back on this day, it was easy to see how the Devil was doing everything he could possibly do to keep us from church that day. It must have felt like the perfect storm to him. He had stressed all of us out to the point of what felt like madness over the welfare of this little baby. And he knew it wouldn't take much more to send us all running back to the house that morning. But God had a little angel by my side that day, and He used her to push me on to where the victory would be delared . . . church.

We arrived late, so I finished wiping my tears and straightened my makeup in the car. We went on in and, because the service had already started, we settled in on the back row and sat toward the end of a pew close by the door.

A few minutes later, I noticed someone else arriving late too. She sat down right beside my daughter, at the end of the pew. I didn't know her, but it was somehow comforting to know I wasn't the only one late for church. I'm sure the Devil didn't want her there that day either.

It wasn't long before the worship music began to shift my emotions. Before I knew it, all I wanted to do was worship. Suddenly, I had come to my senses and realized what was going on, and I knew it was time to rebuke the Devil and tell him to get behind me once again. So I put that old Devil on notice by saying, "Satan, I have come into my Father's house to worship Him and I'm going to worship Him, so get behind me!"

After I'd dealt with him, I lifted my hands toward heaven and began to worship the Lord with all my heart. Not long after I started worshipping the Lord, the woman who also arrived late, tapped me on the shoulder. As I turned, she said, "I have a word for you from the Lord." I was caught a little off guard, so I nodded as if to say, *okay*. Her first words shook me to the core. She said, "The enemy has been tormenting you and your family day and night about the welfare of your unborn child."

Again, I could only nod, as if to say, *yes*! Then she continued on by saying, "He will live and not die. He will be healthy and normal. He will be a joy to you and your family and he will be used of the Lord."

I can't put into words the indescribable joy that flooded my soul after hearing that amazing report from the Lord! She had just read my mail, as we sometimes call prophesying. There was no way she could have known anything about what I was struggling with. Yet every stronghold—all of those old lies we were being told by the enemy—was completely pulled down in that one moment!

The weapons we fight with are not the weapons of the world. On the contrary, they have divine power to demolish strongholds. We demolish arguments and every pretension that sets itself up against the knowledge of God . . . (2 Corinthians 10:4-5).

Again, this passage of scripture explains exactly what happened that day. The enemy's lies were revealed by the Lord with the voice of truth, and the truth brought down every one of the strongholds he'd built up in our minds and was using to torment us. You talk about a hallelujah shout of praise to the Lord! Oh my goodness, I want you to know I walked away from that church service completely free.

So if the Son sets you free, you will be free indeed (John 8:36).

The enemy did everything in his power to keep us from being where God wanted us to be that morning. But, with God's help, the two of us were able to press through the darkness and break free of the Devil's stronghold. Yes, God still had a plan—He used Satan's plans for evil to build our faith to a whole new level that day!

This is why it's so important that we keep pushing through and never stop advancing as we march on through our fiery valley. We must seek Him first, despite our circumstances, or we may never see the victory God has planned for us. So don't get frustrated and turn back when it looks as though hell has you surrounded on all sides. Your victory is just up ahead on the other side of this mountain.

As you might imagine, I couldn't wait to get home and tell my husband what had happened. Everyone was rejoicing and praising God that day! Now that we had God's say so in this matter, I knew it was time for us to stand on it until the very end. As a declaration of our faith, we set up the nursery together as a family, something my husband and I had been putting off out of fear. The pain of taking it down the last time was something we never wanted to experience again. Yes, we were activating our faith and standing on the Word of God, believing it was true. We were going to have a healthy baby boy who would one day be used by the Lord!

But, wouldn't you know it, there was still one last test of our faith to come.

On the day of my youngest son's birth, everything seemed to be going normally. Then, just before he was to be welcomed into the world, his blood pressure started falling.

That was when we saw it. His little purple, lifeless head had the umbilical cord wrapped tightly around his neck, at least two or three times.

The doctor stopped everything as he attempted to cut the baby loose. It felt like he was moving in slow motion. When he made the final cut, my son's lifeless body laid in his hands.

The doctor and the nurse who assisted him lunged into action, starting their life-saving techniques in a frantic attempt to revive him. My husband and I were already praying and standing on the word the Lord had given us for him. By faith, we said, "Lord, You said he would live and not die. We are standing in faith, believing your word of truth." The whole time, the peace of God was upon us as we prayed in faith. Then, suddenly, we watched our lifeless baby boy come back to life.

Yes, we witnessed a miracle right before our eyes as our dead baby son was raised back to life! As we stood on God's promises, God breathed His breath of life into our baby boy.

And that's what faith will do. It brings dead things to life! We did our part and stood on the promises of God by faith, and God did His part and kept His promises. I believe heaven and earth collided that day. You see, *God is not a man, that he should lie* (Numbers 23:19 KJV).

Miracles come through active *faith* in God. Even Jesus couldn't do miracles without others believing with Him in faith. The Bible tells us while Jesus was in His home town, his relatives and the people living there didn't have faith in who He was, therefore *He could not do any miracles there, except lay his hands on a few sick people and heal them* (Mark 6:5-6).

As my husband and I stood together that day on God's promises, my Mother's Day dream came true—by faith! In fact, his birthday often falls on Mother's Day . . . what a great reminder that is. I still tease him and call him my gift that keeps on giving.

Oh, what a joy and a delightful child he was while growing up, just as God said he would be. There were no "terrible twos" or "treacherous threes." He was a complete joy to all our hearts—especially mine. He really was my dream come true child. I remember praying the whole time I was pregnant, "Lord, let him be good."

Because his story is so unique and powerful, I loved to share it any time an opportunity presented itself. However, I soon realized why *Mary treasured up all these things and pondered them in her heart* (Luke 2:19).

You see, the old Devil was listening too, and he knew the prophesy would come to pass if he didn't try to stop it. Any child that is born with the prophesy that they will be used of God already spoken over their life is a huge threat to the kingdom of darkness. Satan already knew the Christ child was born because of the signs foretold by the prophets of His coming birth. He also knew that child would destroy his kingdom of darkness once and for all. Mary was very wise to keep quiet about the child she was carrying.

As I said before, our new little baby boy was just the joy he was prophesied to be. Because of my love for teaching children, I'd already established an active in-home preschool for several years before he was born. It all worked out perfectly, as I was blessed enough to have him and three other students as my last preschool/kindergarten class before sending him off to public school. As he started first grade, I started a new career for myself in real estate.

This was a decision I soon regretted.

Because of my son's God-given, easy-going nature, he was an easy prey for bullies.

Interestingly enough, bullying started early for him, beginning in the third grade, and continued throughout middle school. He was a natural peacemaker, so he never wanted to get into trouble by fighting back. And the last thing he wanted to do was let his parents know what was going on. So, by middle school, the bullying had escalated to the point of cruelty. If you are a parent who has dealt with your child being bullied, then you know how heartbreaking it is to see how it affects their self-esteem.

When he finally did come to us and tell us what was going on, the impact of the rejection and bullying had already taken root in his soul. We went to the school and confronted the problem, but the damage had already eroded his self-esteem. It's so sad that our self-image can be destroyed by others in such a devastating way. Although he knew in his heart from a very early age that he was set apart by God for a special calling, he had lost his true God-given identity. No matter how much we tried to encourage him in the incredibly amazing young man he truly

155

was, he just couldn't see it anymore.

When you have a low self-esteem and desperately want to be accepted, it's easy to fall in with whatever crowd will accept you. Unfortunately, my son found that crowd in the early high school years.

The first thing I noticed was that the friends he chose seemed to be victims of the same low self-image. I didn't blame the kids he was hanging out with, but I did try to get him involved in everything I could think of so that he could meet new people and find new friends. Still, he felt accepted by the group he was in, and that seemed to fill the need every human desires most—being loved just for who they are. Let's face it: Being cool in high school is what seems to matters most to a teenager.

By the time my son was almost eighteen years old, his friends were making many poor choices and he was starting to make them too. Sadly, this wrong crowd was starting to influence his decisions in seriously destructive ways, and I knew any trouble with the law would go on his permanent record. In other words, if God didn't intervene soon, another son's future was about to be destroyed.

I knew in my heart he was just one mistake away from going to jail. Which brings me back to the tipping point I described earlier, when I found myself surrounded on all sides. The best way I can describe it was like being caught in a trap with no way out. My husband worked long hours, and I was still living with and caring for my dying mother, making it even more difficult to keep an eye on him. As I watched helplessly the enemy bore down on me. He'd seen my weakened state and decided to strike while I watched my mother die.

Now you know the depth of my despair during this heart-wrenching time that I spoke about earlier in this chapter. It was then that I fell on my knees and gave a desperate plea for God's divine intervention and help. I cried out to the Lord from the depths of my anguished soul and said, "Lord, I am weary in this battle and I don't know what to do. We're completely surrounded. There seems to be no way out for us. Please, Lord, you see our situation, and you know my heart. Show us what to do!"

In that moment, I fully understood how David felt the day he cried out *Vindicate me, Lord, for I have led a blameless life; I have trusted in the Lord and have not faltered. Test me, Lord, and try me, examine my heart and my mind; for I have always been mindful of your unfailing love and have lived in reliance on your faithfulness* (Psalm 26:1-3).

After praying my prayer of desperation, I didn't hear anything from the Lord in my heart, but I remember feeling led to reach for my Bible. So I did. I was hoping I would hear His voice through His Word. And, sure enough, I did!

Amazingly, the pages seemed to fall open to 2 Chronicles Chapter 20.

As I read the chapter, I quickly discerned that I wasn't just reading another Bible story. I was hearing the voice of the Lord my God and He was giving me a new action plan for my current, overwhelming situation. But it wasn't anything like I was expecting. Oh no, it was better than anything I could have hoped for or imagined. I soon realized that He was speaking to me personally through the events taking place in this chapter of 2 Chronicles. Through these scriptures, He was telling me what to do. In essence, the overall theme of this story was God saying, "Trust Me. I've got this!"

It was absolutely uncanny how the story in 2 Chronicles 20 paralleled with what was going on in our life at that very moment. I could hardly believe my eyes as I read this amazing story. I mean, this was us! All I needed to do was change the various names in the story to ours. As a matter of fact, that's exactly what I felt led to do. So I did. I wrote our names right on the pages of my Bible in the places where it pertained to us.

Now let's get right into the story, and I'll explain the details of the battle plan as we go through by bold typing my thoughts in the places where I interchanged my story with the Bible story, and underlining lines in the text that I found particularly important:

Some people came and told Jehoshaphat, "A vast army is coming against you from Edom, from the other side of the Dead Sea. It is already in Hazezon Tamar" (that is, En Gedi). Alarmed, Jehoshaphat resolved to inquire of the Lord, and he proclaimed a fast for all Judah. The people of Judah came together to seek help from the Lord; indeed, they came from every town in Judah to seek him.

(Yep! All of this sounded very familiar. I, too, was alarmed, and had inquired of the Lord for help. My first battle instructions had been given. It was time to come together with my husband to fast and pray.)

Then Jehoshaphat stood up in the assembly of Judah and Jerusalem at the temple of the Lord in the front of the new courtyard and said:

"Lord, the God of our ancestors, are you not the God who is in heaven? You rule over all the kingdoms of the nations. Power and might are in your hand, and no one can withstand you. Our God, did you not drive out the inhabitants of this land before your people Israel and give it forever to the descendants of Abraham your friend? They have lived in it and have built in it a sanctuary for your Name, saying, 'If calamity comes upon us, whether the sword of judgment, or plague or famine, we will stand in your presence before this temple that bears your Name and will cry out to you in our distress, and you will hear us and save us.'

"But now here are men from Ammon, Moab and Mount Seir, whose territory you would not allow Israel to invade when they came from Egypt; so they turned away from them and did not destroy them. See how they are repaying us by coming to drive us out of the possession you gave us as an inheritance. Our God, will you not judge them? For we have no power to face this vast army that is attacking us. We do not know what to do, but our eyes are on you." **(I had no power left to face this enemy, and I didn't know what to do!)**

All the men of Judah, with their wives and children and little ones, stood there before the Lord.

Then the Spirit of the Lord came on Jahaziel son of Zechariah . . . as he stood in the assembly.

(Then I opened the Word of God, and the Spirit of the Lord came to me and said . . .)

He said: "Listen, King Jehoshaphat and all who live in Judah and Jerusalem!

(Listen, Charlotte and Steve. This is what the Lord says to you.)

This is what the Lord says to you: 'Do not be afraid or discouraged because of this vast army. For the battle is not yours, but God's. *Tomorrow march down against them. They will be climbing up by the Pass of Ziz, and you will find them at the end of the gorge in the Desert of Jeruel.* You will not have to fight this battle. Take up your positions; stand firm and see the deliverance the Lord will give you, Judah and Jerusalem **(Charlotte and Steve)**. Do not be afraid; do not be discouraged. Go out to face them tomorrow, and the Lord will be with you.' "*

Jehoshaphat bowed down with his face to the ground, and all the people of Judah and Jerusalem fell down in worship before the Lord. Then some Levites from the Kohathites and Korahites stood up and praised the Lord, the God of Israel, with a very loud voice.

Early in the morning they left for the Desert of Tekoa. As they set out, Jehoshaphat stood and said, "Listen to me, Judah and people of Jerusalem **(Listen to me, Steve and Charlotte!)**. Have faith in the Lord your God and you will be upheld; have faith in his prophets and you will be successful." *After consulting the people, Jehoshaphat appointed men to sing to the Lord and to praise him for the splendor of his holiness as they went out at the head of the army, saying:*

"Give thanks to the Lord, for his love endures forever."

As they began to sing and praise, the Lord set ambushes against the men of Ammon and Moab and Mount Seir who were invading Judah, and they were defeated. *The Ammonites and Moabites rose up against the men*

159

from Mount Seir to destroy and annihilate them. After they finished slaughtering the men from Seir, they helped to destroy one another.

When the men of Judah came to the place that overlooks the desert and looked toward the vast army, they saw only dead bodies lying on the ground; no one had escaped (2 Chronicles 20:2-24, words in bold are my commentary, underlining is mine).

The Lord confused their enemies and their enemies started destroying each other! God proved good on His promise to His people, and we knew He would prove good on the promises He had made to us that day too.

When you read this chapter, I want to encourage you to replace the names with your names or those in your situation. And each time you read their enemies mentioned, replace it with Satan and/or his army. Do this anytime God gives you a scripture and use it in your prayers. Take it as your own personal word from the Lord.

Because it is!

Again, I believe with all my heart that the day I prayed my prayer of desperation, the tide of the battle turned in our favor.

The very day I call for help, the tide of battle turns. My enemies flee! This one thing I know: God is for me! I am trusting God—oh, praise his promises! (Psalm 56:6-12 TLB).

Remember King David said to Goliath: *it is not by sword or spear that the Lord saves; for the battle is the Lord's* (1 Samuel 17:47). That mighty warrior of God knew God's ways, and he also knew he never fought alone. He always depended on God for help. He said, *Contend LORD, with those who contend with me; fight against those who fight against me* (Psalm 35:1).

Oh yes, the old Devil thought he would get away with his evil plan to destroy my boys' lives, but the Lord saw his evil plot and cast him and his evil forces to the ground!

They expect to get away with it. Don't let them, Lord. In anger cast them to the ground (Psalm 56:7 TLB).

I will never forget how God's Word filled my heart with new hope that day as I finished reading that entire chapter. As I said before, I knew immediately this was our answer to my desperate prayer—a word straight from God Himself. He also let me know what was required of me and my husband, Steve.

You see, like us, King Jehoshaphat was surrounded by a vast army of enemy nations—defeat was imminent. At this point, I was all ears and eyes to see how the Lord was going to deliver His chosen people out of this certain annihilation.

After I finished reading the chapter, I went back and took detailed notes on how they handled this deadly situation. It was then that I clearly understood what the Lord was requiring of us and what our active participation would look like in this battle. Basically, the Lord was letting us know our assignment was to do exactly what He told the people to do. And believe me, we were determined to follow God's leading to the letter.

The first thing King Jehoshaphat did was to proclaim a fast. So, as I stated earlier, we started a fast too.

Next, everyone, including the king, came before God to seek His help through prayer. So we prayed and sought the Lord for His divine help also.

Then King Jehoshaphat stood up before the Temple of the Lord as all the people were gathered around. He began to acknowledge who God was, and His rule over all the nations. He went on to let God know that he knew that, even as a king, he did not have all power and might, but that all power and might were in God's hands. He reminded the Lord of their obedience to Him. He reminded the Lord that He had given that land to them as an inheritance as promised through Abraham.

So we too began to acknowledge and praise God as the all-powerful

God that He was, and expressed our inability to fight these demon forces that were surrounding us alone. Then we reminded Him of the promises He had made to us if we raised our children to serve Him, and the blood covenant we had entered into with Jesus, His divine Son. God you said, *"As for me, this is my covenant with them," says the Lord. "My Spirit, who is on you, will not depart from you, and my words that I have put in your mouth will always be on your lips, on the lips of your children and on the lips of their descendants—from this time on and forever," says the Lord* (Isaiah 59:21).

Jesus Christ is the mediator of the New Covenant, and His death on the cross is the basis of this promise.

In the same way, after the supper he took the cup, saying, "This cup is the new covenant in my blood, which is poured out for you (Luke 22:20).

That was also the day I made my new declaration of faith. I said with David, *I remain confident of this: I will see the goodness of the Lord in the land of the living* (Psalm 27:13).

I found myself quoting this scripture over and over again, by faith, believing it would one day come to pass.

Jehoshaphat went on in his prayer, reminding God of the promises He had made to protect them if they were obedient to do what He commanded them. What he basically said was, *Lord, we kept our part of the deal and we are counting on You to keep Yours.* Yes, he was reminding God that they belonged to Him, and he was counting on God to come through for them. And as His children, we knew we had the same right to count on Him too . . . so we did.

As you read Jehoshaphat's prayer, it's clear to see in the way he approached God and in the words that he spoke that he had a very close and personal relationship with the Lord. We too have this same close personal relationship with God the Father, through His Son Jesus. I knew how important it was to keep my personal relationship with the Lord strong, so I continually devoted myself to His Word and prayer.

Now please understand, if you didn't raise your children to live for Christ because you found Him later in life, God still loves them! And you too, for that matter. They are still His children and so are you. Also, because you are a believer, you are anointed to stand in the gap for your children. So stand in faith believing God for your breakthrough just as I did—you have every right as a born-again believer to stand in the same faith, because you carry the same power and authority through Christ.

Though my children had fallen away from the truth, I knew in my heart He would go after them and rescue them because of His great mercy. Jesus said, *Suppose one of you has a hundred sheep and loses one of them. Doesn't he leave the ninety-nine in the open country and go after the lost sheep until he finds it?* (Luke 15:4).

Are you seeing the pattern? I hope so!

God is a promise keeper.

King Jehoshaphat knew it, and I knew it too.

I think this scripture was my favorite part of King Jehoshaphat's prayer:

We do not know what to do, but our eyes are on you. (2 Chronicles 20:12).

Wow! That was me. I was completely clueless the day I cried out to God, and I needed to hear from Him desperately. The words *I don't know what to do, but my eyes are on you* rang out in my soul. I was reminded once again in that moment to keep my eyes on the Lord. And that is exactly what I did as I fasted and prayed in the days leading up to the final victory. I would often say those very words to the Lord. *Lord, I don't know what to do, but my eyes are on You.* It was my way of finding comfort and hope—I was letting Him know I was in complete surrender to His perfect will and His perfect plan for our lives. I was counting on Him entirely to rescue us. I had seen Him do miracles before on the day He raised my lifeless baby boy back to life, and even in my imprisoned son's life too. And I was fully expecting Him to do it again. In my heart,

I just knew God was going to use what the enemy intended for evil and destruction for our good.

Once again, my husband and I would stand in faith believing. Just like we did at his birth. Oh yes, we had been given our next assignment, and we were determined to do exactly what the tribe of Judah did to get our victory too.

***

As I continued to read the chapter in 2 Chronicles, it suddenly dawned on me what God was saying to us—the battle was not even ours . . . *it was His*!

Do not be afraid or discouraged because of this vast army. For the battle is not yours, but God's (2 Chronicles 20:15).

I'll never forget that exhilarating moment; the Lord was taking over this fight, and all we had to do was trust Him. Yes, the Commander of Heaven's Armies saw our hopeless situation, and He was making a way out for us where there seemed to be absolutely no way out! Yes, our God was stepping in front of us and He was going before us!

The Lord himself goes before you and will be with you; he will never leave you nor forsake you. Do not be afraid; do not be discouraged (Deuteronomy 31:8).

Our new word from God had victory written all over it. One thing was for certain, we knew from our previous battles that our God never loses a battle!

The Lord will fight for you; you need only to be still (Exodus 14:14).

Without a doubt, God is always fighting for us and He wants us to be active in the fight with Him. As I have said before, He expects the redeemed of the earth to join forces by faith with Him and fight for their loved ones . . . with Him by our side.

In my excitement, I realized I was once again standing at a new door. I was so fired up in that moment, and ready to participate in any way God instructed me. I couldn't wait to get armored up and head into battle with the Lord at my right hand! I knew in my heart we had the victory if we would believe and follow His instruction to the letter.

Oh yes, God was getting ready to rescue us once again from the raging sea:

He reached down from on high and took hold of me; he drew me out of deep waters. He rescued me from my powerful enemy, from my foes, who were too strong for me. They confronted me in the day of my disaster, but the Lord was my support. He brought me out into a spacious place; he rescued me because he delighted in me (2 Samuel 22:17-20).

I believe it was during that very moment, as we stood firm in our faith, having done everything we could to stand, God said to Satan, *Satan, this time it's you and Me; leave my daughter and her family out of this!*

Having done all . . . stand (Ephesians 6:13 KJV).

Sometimes you just need to be still and stand the Devil down by not moving a muscle while he comes charging at you. He says, *"Be still, and know that I am God.* (Psalm 46:10) As the redeemed of the Lord, we don't have to run from an inferior foe. We are to carry out our orders and keep advancing the kingdom of God by fulfilling the assignment He has given us. Firmly stand your ground, my friend, and take back what the enemy has stolen from you; take your children back by faith, they still belong to you, they are a gift that was given to you from the Lord:

Children are a gift from the Lord; they are a reward from him (Psalm 127:3 NLT).

It's time to get violent with the powers of hell and take back what the enemy has stolen from our families. *From the days of John the Baptist until now, the kingdom of Heaven has been forcefully advancing...* (Matthew 11:12) So if that means spiritual warfare, then let's get in the heat of the battle, right on the frontlines with our warrior God! Our Lord Jesus Christ is an overcoming, conquering warrior King, and He is training up warriors who will fight along beside Him. He says, *The Lord will fight for you; you need only to be still* (Exodus 14:14). That's God's way of saying, *I'm in the fight with you; I'm fighting for you, not against you! Therefore, settle down your soul, your emotions, and your mind, and trust Me!*

I believe God is mobilizing His earthly army for battle in these last days, therefore, He must prepare us for the battle. And because He doesn't fight using weapons of this world, He is using our current struggles to train us in the way we should use these divine weapons. We're in a spiritual war all right, and those on the earth are His ground troops who operate in the spirit realm with Him by faith! We can see from reading God's Word that our faith activates the heavenly realms and calls them forth into action!

We see Jehoshaphat mobilizing God's earthly army on the ground, but he doesn't give them carnal earthly battle instruction; he gives them spiritual warfare instructions, in the exact same way God has been giving us spiritual instructions through His Word.

After consulting the people, Jehoshaphat appointed men to sing to the Lord and to praise him for the splendor of his holiness as they went out at the head of the army, saying: "Give thanks to the Lord, for his love endures forever" (2 Chronicles 20:21).

They went out singing their victory song, believing by faith that the victory was already theirs! Can you see how all this works? Nevertheless, can you imagine commanders today using this battle strategy? God always does things His own way. That's why He says, *For My thoughts are not your thoughts, neither are your ways my ways* (Isaiah 55:8).

Moses said, *If you are pleased with me, teach me your ways so I may know you and continue to find favor with you* (Exodus 33:13). God wants us to know Him and His ways. That's why He tells us we must renew our minds by washing them in His Word. Then we will know how He operates in the heavenly realm as we walk out on the battlefield in peace with His favor resting upon us.

Do not conform to the pattern of this world, but be transformed by the renewing of your mind. Then you will be able to test and approve what God's will is—his good, pleasing and perfect will (Romans 12:2).

God doesn't think like the world—the world doesn't know Him. And He doesn't want us thinking like the world either. If we do, we will never win the spiritual battles that are sure to come our way. Why? Because He alone knows what Satan is up to in that very moment, and we can know it too if we will seek His face. Then we can activate all of heaven by using the faith-filled words He gives us to fight back against the onslaughts of the evil one.

If we are serious about pleasing Him and having a close personal relationship with Him, then we will prove it to Him by seeking Him first in every area of our lives. To seek means to go in search of or in quest of. I was in a desperate search for answers when my family came under attack, and I went on a quest for those answers from the only One who had the true answers.

Are you on a quest to know God and His divine Son Jesus? How about the Holy Spirit? They are all God! It's up to us to seek out this mystery and let Him reveal it to us.

You will seek me and find me when you seek me with all your heart (Jeremiah 29:13).

Again, God will give us the answers to our prayers *if* we will seek Him with our whole hearts. If we want the victory, it's up to us to do the seeking. Yes, we have a part to play in all of this if we want to live a victorious life, reigning with God.

Our Almighty God is so amazing, He does things in His own unique and mysterious way. I love to read the stories of old and watch how God works in the spiritual realm. We may live on planet earth with fleshly bodies, but there is an unseen spiritual war going on all around us. Every day, God is trying to teach us how to join in the fight that's going on in this unseen spiritual world around us. The visible destructions from this fight are obvious, but soon as we join in the fight, the restoration is just as obvious!

Again, when we read about God's battle plans in His Word, it's never the way we would consider fighting. We see this clearly as we watch how the king followed God's instructions by commanding the warrior praise team to go out in front of the army and sing praises to the Lord. As crazy as that may sound to us, and I'm sure it may have sounded at the time to the king too, nonetheless, we don't hear about the king arguing with the Lord about it. He just followed orders. As I say that, I'm reminded of what Joshua did when He inquired of the Lord for battle instructions. In Judges 20:18, we see Joshua leading the Israelites to Bethel before going into battle. There, they inquired of the Lord, asking: *"Who of us is to go up first to fight against the Benjamites?" The Lord replied, "Judah shall go first."*

But why Judah? Because Judah was the tribe of praise!

Do you see what God was asking them to do? He was instructing them to rejoice and praise Him *now*, before the battle was fought. He was letting them know it was time to start living in the victory by faith and singing their victory praise song. If you want to conquer the enemy, you must start by praising God first! Now you know why God told me to live in the victory at the beginning of my journey, and why He instructed me to rejoice from the very beginning through songs of victory! Although I didn't have a full understanding at that time of how very powerful my victory songs were, I certainly do now! That's why I just had to write this book—people need words of hope like this, especially in the dark valley, where it's hard to find hope. I wanted everyone to know how amazing the God I serve was. His story just had to be told! Faith in God is trusting Him completely for what we hope for and cannot yet see. Let's face it, if we can see it, then it's not faith at all!

Now faith is confidence in what we hope for and assurance about what we do not see (Hebrews 11:1).

Think about it: 2 Chronicles 20 goes on to say: *As they began to sing and praise, the Lord set ambushes against the men of Ammon and Moab and Mount Seir* (Satan and his demons of darkness) *who were invading Judah, and they were defeated* (2 Chronicles 20:22, parenthetical thoughts are mine).

Keep in mind what happened that day. The Word says, *as they began to sing and praise.* Not *after* several rounds of the same chorus, but *as they began* to sing and praise, the Lord set ambushes and their enemies were annihilated! They set the hand of God in motion when they took that first step forward by faith and started singing the first words of their victory song!

Is God trying to show us something here? I believe so. I know when I was in the heat of our fiery fight, I sang the same song they did. As I sang *my* victory song to the top of my lungs, I *believed* our enemies were being annihilated. Then I just sat back and tried to imagine the enemies of my soul being wiped out by the Commander of Heaven's Armies and His mighty angel warriors. For me, the day I read this story, I knew it was going to be a glorious day of victory as I activated God's plan. I claimed it as my own, believing by faith it was mine. I declared with all that was within me, *WE HAVE WON! THE ENEMY HAS BEEN DEFEATED, AND THE LAMB HAS OVERCOME THIS DAY!*

Praise God, it wasn't long after following my new battle instructions and giving my declaration of faith that I saw the victory unfolding before my eyes. I could also see how our time of fervent prayer and fasting had paid off as we walked through this amazing new open door by faith. We didn't see a miracle take place that day—actually, for a short time, things seemed to get much worse. Yes, the battle raged on for a while, but we stood in faith and waited for our next set of orders, even as it reached a climax. Or, you might say, a turning point. It was at that turning point that we would be given our most difficult orders yet, as the Lord gave us His clear directions in what to do in our youngest son's situation.

Little did we know that when we walked through that door to

169

participate in the battle there would be one final and *enormous* test of faith waiting on the other side, one in which we would need to carry out to the letter. As a matter of fact, when I told my husband what the Lord had instructed us to do, even he wasn't sure if he would be strong enough in his faith to carry it out. Nevertheless, we knew it was a clear word from the Lord, and we had to do our part and follow orders no matter how unsettling they were at the time.

I wish I could give you more details about this, however, in order to protect our youngest son's future, I can't share details related to this gut-wrenching test. But I will tell you, those who have heard the story in full detail know it was only by the amazing grace of God that we were able to pass this final test. To be completely honest, it stretched our faith to an all new level as God asked us once again to trust Him completely with the son we had already laid down on the altar of God's will.

Amazingly enough, right after we went through with what God told us to do, we saw miracles happen. Miracles that would have never taken place if we would have done anything differently than what God instructed us to do. I must admit, at that time, it felt like we were walking once again with our Lord, inside the fiery furnace. Even so, Jesus gave us the strength we needed to do it! His peace was like a mighty fortress surrounding us and keeping us strong and steadfast throughout the days and months that followed. Just like so many times before, our awesome God came through in a way that was exceedingly and abundantly above anything we could have ever hoped, thought, or imagined.

Now to him who is able to do immeasurably more than all we asked or imagined, according to his power that is at work within us, to him be glory (Ephesians 3:20-21).

Yes, once again, our God was faithful to turn the tide of the battle in our favor and get our young son back on the right road—the road that led to a complete and amazing victory! As I said before, that victory didn't come over night, but by taking one step of faith after another as we advance toward the victor's circle. Looking back now, nearly six years later, I can honestly say, God literally saved our youngest son's future and the promise God had given us that he would be used by the Lord. We'll always be grateful and never forget how our gracious Lord *once again* brought another son's dead, dry bones back to life!

Today, our son is attending college and pursuing a career in nursing. He is living for the Lord with all his heart as he helps others overcome the same demons he once fought and defeated. Although he was bullied in his young life, when he was in the fight of his life, the Warrior Spirit of God rose up inside of him and defeated the giant of all bullies! Oh yes, the Warrior Holy Spirit living inside of him not only got him back to his spiritual roots, but taught him how to fight back using God's supernatural weapons of mass destruction.

I waited patiently for the Lord; he turned to me and heard my cry. He lifted me out of the slimy pit, out of the mud and mire . . . He put a new song in my mouth (Psalm 40:1-3).

13

Sing Your Victory Songs

Sing to him a new song . . . and shout for joy (Psalm 33:3).

Oh yes, I'm singing and shouting it from the rooftops! I'm not going to keep it shrouded in darkness, as the enemy would have me to. Oh no, I'm shining God's light into the darkness and exposing his evil plans for all to see! That old devil has messed with the wrong Mama's child this time! *O clap your hands, all ye people; shout unto God with the voice of triumph* (Psalm 47:1 KJV).

It's time to start singing your triumphant victory song mamas and daddies! Sing it and activate the heavenly realm with your faith-filled songs of praise; then watch the walls of fear, doubt, and worry start falling down. Come along beside your conquering King and watch the mountain move as you trust Him to fight your battles for you. May this be your finest hour, as you lay everything you treasure most in this life down on the mercy seat of God and surrender your will to His perfect and good will.

Jesus said, *Yet I want your will to be done, not mine* (Luke 22:42 NLT).

Our example is Jesus. He is the Lord of the battle, the one who wants to fight our battles for us. Let Him be the Lord of all in your life today and watch His mountain-moving power unfold right before your eyes!

We're not going to wait until we have the victory to rejoice; we're going to rejoice in song now, knowing the victory is ours!

What an easy and effective way to fight back against the evil one. I mean, you can do it throughout your day for the most part. Praising without ceasing—another form of prayer.

In this chapter, and other chapters throughout this book, you have seen how powerfully God uses singing, by faith, to bring forth amazing breakthroughs and powerful results. What a power-filled weapon!

This battle plan may have some of you standing at another new door. Nevertheless, I hope you will at least put it in your armor belt. Without a doubt, it was one of my best and most effective God-given battle strategies. Not only would it calm my nerves almost immediately, but it also helped settle my entire being and restore my focus.

The thing I loved most about singing along with my favorite Christian radio station was how the Lord would make sure I was singing just the right song to defeat whatever demon I was up against at that moment. It was just the perfect weapon for the breakthrough I needed to help me change the "worry channel" that was going through my mind to the "praise channel" of God. I'd suddenly find myself in a whole new place with renewed spiritual fervor and even a stronger resolve to win!

Oh, yes, singing took me to another place, spiritually speaking. It helped me to change my focus and get me back to my set place of victory. Before long, my attention was no longer on the circumstances of that day or the past, but on the eyes of my Lord. I found that God was doing a new thing in my heart through music, and I perceived it to be just the weapon I needed in my armor belt to make my way through the wilderness valley and on into my Promised Land.

See, I am doing a new thing! Now it springs up; do you no perceive it? I am making a way in the wilderness and streams in the wasteland (Isaiah 43:19).

Oh, trust me, I knew full well there were demons surrounding me on every side in the spirit realm, but I made a conscious decision to sing my way through the wilderness. Those songs brought me to His streams of refreshing. And I knew my faith songs would bless the Lord and let Him know I was still in the fight with Him. Even on my darkest days, I sang a song of praise to the Lord by faith.

Through Jesus, therefore, let us continually offer to God a sacrifice of praise—the fruit of lips that openly profess his name (Hebrews 13:15).

Trust me when I say, I didn't always feel joyful, let alone like bursting into song; still, it was during those most difficult moments that I sang my victory songs as a sacrifice of praise. In my spirit, I knew that as I gave my sacrifice of praise by faith, my God was defeating the enemies of my soul! I could actually *feel* my joy start rising up as I sang in faith, believing and trusting that during this most difficult time, God was still fighting for me. As I said before, in my mind, as I sang, I would visualize the demons being defeated on my behalf.

Not only did I find that singing was one of God's most powerful weapons of spiritual warfare as I journeyed through the dark wilderness valley, I also discovered that singing would profoundly alter my inner soul. Yes, it took me to another place, a place above the storm where the eagles soar effortlessly. When the Lord first showed me how powerful this weapon was, He also encouraged me to make singing a part of my shield of faith. Whenever I was flooded with one horrific situation after another or fearful thoughts from the enemy, I would put up my shield of song and deflect those fiery darts by singing a praise song to the Lord.

Again, the enemy knows just where to strikes his evil blows— directly into our souls! According to the Word of God, your soul is basically *you*. Your personality, who you are. It consists of your mind (intellect), your feelings (emotions), and your will (what you are willing to do). When you sing, all these parts of your soul are profoundly altered. That's why the Word of God tells us to put on a garment of praise—it drives out the spirit of despair. It's like putting up a shield or garment to protect your soul (heart).

The book of Isaiah says He will give us *the oil of joy instead of mourning, and a garment of praise instead of a spirit of despair* (Isaiah 61:3). When we're going through this time of loss, it can feel as though we are mourning a death. I remember grieving over the dreams I thought were gone forever in my son's life. At first I didn't understand why I was mourning, but loss is loss, and it doesn't matter what the loss is, we still grieve. I'm so thankful that God has already provided us with His amazing oil of joy and garment of praise through the many anointed praise songs He has given us to sing. When feelings of despair wash over our soul, we can guard our hearts by putting on our garment of praise (our shield). The next thing you know, God is pouring out His oil of joy right onto your soul. This is one way God pours out His oil of joy and covers us in His protective peace.

Sometimes all you need to sing is His Holy name—*Jesus!*

The name of the LORD is a fortified tower; the righteous run to it and are safe (Proverbs 18:10).

Oh yes, His name is a fortified tower that we can run into and be safe from our enemies. This is a powerful weapon, and when used in songs of praise by faith, it's like a sweet-smelling aroma to the nostrils of God. An incense of praise, just like our prayers:

May my prayer be set before you like incense (Psalm 141:2).

Singing guards your heart by filling your mind and emotions with God's supernatural, transcending peace—a peace that, because of your circumstances in the natural, shouldn't be there at all, yet it goes beyond your natural understanding . . . because it's *super*natural.

And the peace of God, which transcends all understanding, will guard your hearts and your minds in Christ Jesus (Philippians 4:7).

As we sing, we actively release His peace and loose His manifested presence in our spirits. His presence brings with it the power needed to remove the heavy spirit of fear, dread, and sorrow that comes from the evil one. It's the supernatural touch of God that will guard your heart and keep you from going into that dark place where the spirit of despair dwells.

I can't stress enough how powerful this supernatural weapon of singing can be as you travel through the demon-filled valley. As I say that, I'm reminded of when my theme song came out on the radio. Yep, right in the middle of the war, the Lord wrote a song just for me. Or, at least it felt like it was written just for me. The song is "The Same God," written by a band called New Song . . . How about that! The encouraging message in the song lets us know that the same God who was with us going into the battle will still be with us as we're coming out.

Can you see why it was my special song? What are the odds that a song would be written at that very time saying exactly what I needed to hear! I bet you can say the same thing about some of your theme songs too. Songs that lift your soul to new heights and confirm that He is there.

I was once again reminded by this encouraging song that the same God who was dancing with me on the mountaintop was the same God with me now in the drudgery of the valley below. He alone would lead me out of this dark, evil place. What a timely and beautiful reminder that my God was still with me and standing at my right hand.

"I, the LORD, have called you in righteousness; I will take hold of your hand (Isaiah 42:6). And why did He take hold of my hand and lead me through this dark valley? So I could be used as a vessel for God, a light for those who were sure to come after me . . . to free captives from prison and to release from the dungeon those who sit in darkness (Isaiah 42:7). This scripture is talking about Jesus. Isn't that why Jesus came, to set us free and light the way? Now He's sending us and asking , "Whom shall I send? And who will go for us?" And I said, "Here am I. Send me!" (Isaiah 6:8).

Yes, one day even before the war even began, I heard His call and responded with the same answer that Isaiah did. "Here am I. Send me!"

Have you ever thought about what would be required of you as a follower of Jesus Christ? The day I heard His voice and answered His call, I must say I had no idea how much that response would cost me. Nevertheless, I meant it with all my heart and, I must say, I'm so glad Jesus sent me! Because now I'm singing my new song to inspire and encourage those who are sitting in valleys of darkness and sorrow. God said: *I will lead the blind by ways they have not known, along unfamiliar paths I will guide them; I will turn the darkness into light before them and make the rough places smooth. These are the things I will do; I will not forsake them* (Isaiah 42:16).

Our story of victory is our song! Yes, we're the sent ones, those God trusted to fulfill His greater purpose. It's time to *make a joyful noise unto the Lord, all the earth: make a loud noise, and rejoice, and sing praise* (Psalm 98:4 KJV). This verse tells me that God enjoys our joyful praising and singing, even if it sounds like a loud noise to everyone else. I'm sure my new song sounds like a loud and annoying song to the Devil! All the more reason to sing it to anyone who needs to hear words of hope. One thing I know, the Lord enjoys the sound of it . . . and so do all those who need encouragement! Yes, my friend, our testimonies are songs of refreshment to those who are sitting in dark places that feel like dungeons with no way out. Our songs of hope set the captives free!

The Word of God tells us He works in ways we cannot see. This is so true. I don't need my natural eyes to know when He is moving in my heart. His presence and the effect of what He is doing in my soul as I enter into joyful praise and worship says it all. I'm sure if you've been faithfully following the Lord for very long, you've experienced this too. Suddenly we realize that our Lord's oil of joy has soaked into our very souls, and it covers us like a sweet, soft garment. Before long, our weary faces smile again with a joyful glow as He lifts us up to where we belong—seated once again with Him. No wonder we get the victory over the evil one through singing God's songs of praise and worship.

Keep in mind, it's one of the easiest weapons to access at a second's notice. Especially if you've already been in the habit of doing it.

When we stop the madness of our day and remember where we belong by singing our praise songs here on earth, I believe we are instantly joined with the ongoing chorus in the heavenly realms that sing around the throne of God. My friend, God is asking you to live from your set place, right now, and to trust Him to be the God He says He is. Join in with the angelic choir and sing!

Then suddenly there appeared with the angel a multitude of the heavenly host (angelic army) praising God and saying, "Glory to God in the highest [heaven], and on earth peace among men with whom He is well-pleased" (Luke 2: 13-14, AMP).

You've just got to love those *suddenly* moments from God! You never know when they will come—you could just be lying in your bed or on a hillside, like the shepherds—but whenever or wherever they come . . . you are never the same again!

Have you had a few of those moments? If so, dwell on them often and encourage yourself in the Lord with those heavenly thoughts of inspiration. Especially in dark hours of sorrow and sadness. Refocus your mind and watch how His light starts bursting through that darkness.

Every time you sing a song by faith or give a testimony of praise to God, you are using your overcoming power to defeat the evil one. Your song to the Lord is a testimony of praise and a declaration of your faith and loving devotion to Him . . . it's your overcoming testimony of praise that breaks through the darkest night. That's right, whether you're praising Him by giving a spoken testimony or by singing a song, to Him it's all a beautiful medley of praise. The Bible says, *Our lives are a Christ-like fragrance rising up to God* (2 Corinthians 2:15 NLT).

And they overcame him by the blood of the Lamb, and the word of their testimony; (Revelation 12:11 KJV).

Have you ever sat and listened to some of the powerful words in those anointed songs you've heard? Did you know most of those songs are incredible personal testimonies of God's faithfulness in the darkest valleys of the artist's life. Many artists promise not to relent in their faithfulness to God, even if it means death. You can tell when a song is birthed out of pain—it's like a personal proclamation to all of heaven, letting God know they are trusting Him no matter what. We must have that same attitude, and a willingness to trust Him explicitly in the most severe storms of our lives.

Words can't express how extremely grateful I am that I learned about this weapon of singing and praising in my earliest battles. I quickly realized this was God's way of working in ways I could not see. One thing was for sure, He was constantly reaffirming His wonder-working power as I sang and gave Him praise. It didn't take long for me to realize He was going to use this weapon throughout the demon-possessed valley, until we all safely reached the other side. My testimony and declaration of faith being expressed through songs that came straight from my heart soon became a way of life for me. (Again, can't you just imagine how annoying that was for the Devil!)

My new songs of praise brought with them a steadfast, joyful, and overcoming life! A newness of life in which I no longer went around looking beat down and defeated. Let's face it: I couldn't reflect my Savior's glory if I was singing a song of defeat to everyone who would listen. How sad would that be? Unfortunately, many believers fall into that pit of despair and never reach their Promised Land. They just keep wandering through the wilderness, and yet they don't understand why. But God never intended for us to live there—not *His* children! Would you want your children living like that? Of course not. You would do everything in your power to convince them of who they really are and how much they're dearly loved.

Yes, we all have bad days when our crosses seem to weigh us down. I have had countless times where I felt as though I was bent beneath the load. Even so, it's during those times we need to grab hold of the Word of God and get His words of encouragement and praise on our lips through war-ship songs. When we do this, spiritually speaking, we keep advancing and marching forward, through the wilderness battlefield, just like the soldiers of God in 2 Chronicles 20!

There was one thing I couldn't help but notice as I sang my way through each battle: it wasn't long before I found myself winning the battle and singing a *new* victory song! New spiritual strength seemed to rise up in me as I defeated one giant after the other.

Wasn't that the same thing that gave King David the confidence that he could defeat the giant Goliath too? Just think of the dark valley as a place of warrior training for eventually defeating the final giant and winning the overall war!

Again, I'm not saying I never had challenging days—bad ones—where I collapsed on the valley floor. I experienced many of those days too. I'll never forget the day I fell on my knees at the altar in church one Sunday morning, completely defeated. Nevertheless, I got back up that day, revived and ready, once again, for battle. Yes, I knew what to do . . . run to the mercy seat of God!

My friend, I know if He did these things for me, raising me up time and time again, He will certainly do the same for you. You see, the Word of God says that our *God is no respecter of persons.* (Acts 10:34 KJV) If I was able to remain stable and vital in the fight as I learned from the Master how to live in my set place of victory with Him, you can too! What He did for me, I promise He will do for you.

Therefore, sing, sing, sing your victory songs! It works . . . believe me. I'm a witness to its power. Praise Him in your darkest hour; sing through the fiercest storm songs of praise, filled with faith. While you're at it, lift your holy hands and clap, giving a shout *with the voice of triumph.* He is fighting for you and with you!

Psalm 134:2 says, *Lift up your hands in the sanctuary and bless the Lord. And in Psalm 47:1, O clap your hands, all ye people; shout unto God with the voice of triumph* (KJV). I love to lift my hands and praise God in church. I'm not ashamed, nor should you be—it's biblical!

The Bible is filled with verses that tell of people who loved the Lord lifting up holy hands while singing songs of praise to His Holy name. They praised their God loudly and unashamedly, using the talents He had given them to sing and play musical instruments. All of this praise was to bring glory to God alone. King David not only wrote many of the songs about his victories in Psalms, but he even danced before Him with all his might while singing and praising his Lord God for another great victory. He didn't care what others thought; he was filled with an attitude of gratefulness, and all he wanted to do was bring glory to God for His faithfulness.

So don't worry about those around you and what they're thinking; God will deal with their thoughts and attitudes if they're foolish enough to judge you. Don't let them hold you back from giving God the praise He deserves. You have an audience of One—the Holy One!

Have you ever noticed that those who are leading worship on stage seem to be overflowing with joy? Well, now you know why. Join in with all your heart and sing! Lift up His holy name with praise and thanksgiving and watch how He lifts your soul with His oil of overflowing joy.

Another example of the power of music and song being used against the evil one was seen when the first king of Israel, Saul, used music to send tormenting evil spirits running. We see this in 1 Samuel 16:23:

Then Saul sent word to Jesse, saying, "Allow David to remain in my service, for I am pleased with him."...David would take up his lyre and play. Then relief would come to Saul; he would feel better, and the evil spirit would leave him.

As you can see here, an evil spirit brought with it fear and torment, but music brought relief when David played, because he was anointed by God to play musical instruments and sing. That's why it's so important to listen to good, anointed Christian music—like King David, God has personally gifted and anointed those artists to minister to you through their God-given talents of music and songs. So join in with them and send those tormenting demons running, just like David did!

The Word of God says, *and the yoke shall be destroyed because of the anointing* (Isaiah 10:27 KJV). The yoke, as referred to here, was a form of bondage. God's anointing on godly Christian music breaks off the yoke of bondage. An evil spirit brings bondage. Only God can anoint a person to have this kind of special ability and gifting. With that anointing comes the power to break off an evil spirit that has attached itself to someone. The secret is to run the spirit off before it attaches to you and causes despair. The short of it is, evil spirits can't stand the sound of godly, anointed music and songs of praise.

In Psalm 28:7, the psalmist wrote, *The Lord is my strength and my shield; my heart trusts in him, and he helps me. My heart leaps for joy, and with my song I praise him.* When we trust God through faith, we can feel His ever-present shield around us, and that's why our hearts leap with joy as we sing praises to Him.

But you, LORD, are a shield around me, my glory, the One who lifts my head high (Psalm 3:3).

Can you see from reading these verses what the enemy is up to when he torments you with worry and fear? He's after your joy . . . which is *your strength*!

Do not grieve, for the joy of the LORD is your strength (Nehemiah 8:10).

Keep in mind, if the Devil sends his evil spirit to discourage you and attach his evil spirit of fear to you, you become weak, thus, an easy target to defeat. I believe that's why God tell us to put on a garment of praise for the spirit of heaviness. Think about it. When that thing gets attached to you, you are carrying around an old, heavy demon. Knock him right off your back with a praise song. You don't have to put up with that; you're a child of the Most High God, for heaven's sake!

Just sing. As I said before, in God's ears, it's beautiful, because you are singing to Him in faith, believing He is fighting your battles for you. Yes, God is listening and, believe me, Satan is listening too. We know from reading God's holy Word that they're both gathered here with us on this battleground called earth!

But woe to the earth . . . because the devil has gone down to you! (Revelation 12:12).

Yes, he is here, and we are his target. Therefore we must learn to fight back. He hates us because of God's great love for us, and he won't stop until he destroys all that God loves, if that were possible. Let's not make it possible for him to grieve God's heart because we weren't willing to do our part in the battle.

My friend, I want to remind you again that you are in a war, and the only way to win a war is to fight! You will need to use every spiritual weapon God has made available to make it to the Promised Land. Search out powerful battle songs. Pray that God will give you many demon-destroying songs during your battle. Again, it will be your greatest and easiest weapon of warfare . . . so *use it*!

I will never forget the time I desperately needed to sing a warfare song: my youngest son was under a severe attack and I'd just received word. At the time, I was with a really big client of mine. This attack came during our 2 Chronicles 20 experience. Again, this was a fierce battle, at this time the enemy was trying desperately to sabotage what God was doing in our youngest son's life. Keep in mind, as I said before, the enemy knows just when to attack, and it won't always be convenient to sing your battle songs or get down on your knees to pray. But you can always pray and sing silently in your heart. Remember, if you can worry silently, you can pray silently, and you can sing silently too! God hears you when you call!

I prayed to the Lord, and he answered me. He freed me from all my fears (Psalm 34:4 NLT).

Once again, I overcame the spirit of fear through songs of praise and won the battle Satan started that day. Remember that wars are fought one battle at a time; you may not win them all, but never surrender, because with the Lord on your side, the final victory will be yours!

God often gave King David new songs after many of his battles. Just read Psalms; you'll not only find them, but you will be encouraged by them. Many of the songs he wrote were written during or after a vicious, bloody battle. He knew and understood the powerful weapon called singing. I know there isn't scripture to back this theory up, but I wouldn't be surprised if he led his men in song as they raced into their many battles.

David is described in the Bible as one of the greatest warriors of all time and a man after God's own heart. I don't know about you, but I want to be in that crowd of great warriors too! Again, I want to encourage you to listen to your favorite Christian music if you aren't already, and let the Lord put a *war*-ship (worship) song in your heart every day. Start writing down the most powerful ones that deeply minister to you; sing them as a declaration of the victory God is going to give you. Let them be your battle cry of faith!

Obviously, singing drives the enemy crazy! He won't stay around long if you start that stuff! And what a great way to send him running. The Word of God tells us to make a melody in our heart to the Lord and to sing His praises, *speaking to yourselves in psalms and hymns and spiritual songs, singing and making melody in your heart to the Lord* (Ephesians 5:19 KJV). Sometimes, this is the only way you can talk yourself out of the trouble you're in.

The valley is dark and there are many pitfalls along the way because of the darkness. But you can talk yourself out of that pit of darkness by singing songs that bring forth life and light. Praise Him and tell Him of His wonderful faithfulness. Great is His faithfulness! Give Him the praise; He deserves. And watch the spirit of heaviness lift as you do.

The Lord Jesus gave me many praise songs during my journey. But there was one that deeply ministered to my heart. It was written by Lawrence Chewning (later reworked and performed by Ray Boltz) Chewning wrote this song while going through a time of great loss. The song is called "*The Anchor Holds*," and it talks about how our dreams and visions often pass through our hands like grains of sand.

Isn't that how our life is sometimes? We have dreams and visions for our children and loved ones, but when we're in the storm, they seem to slip right through our hands. Don't let your visions and dreams die. Stand in faith believing God will bring them to pass . . . even in your lifetime. Use what the enemy intended for evil—to destroy you—for good.

I can't tell you the times I sang this song, with tears running down my checks. Again, it ministered deeply to me, especially during my darkest days. Because I knew that, despite having been battered and torn, God's anchor never stopped holding me as I faced the raging sea. No matter how difficult the storm, the anchor of my soul continued to hold me (hold my hand), in spite of the storm. Jesus is that anchor that holds and never let's go. Just reach out and take hold of His hand! I did that many times—I would literally reach out my hand as if I were taking the Lord's hand, just to remind myself that He was right beside me. It was my way of strengthening myself in the Lord, as I walked out of the valley of discouragement.

Did you know the Scriptures tell us that God sings over us?

The Lord your God is with you, the Mighty Warrior who saves. He will take great delight in you; in his love he will no longer rebuke you, but will rejoice over you with singing (Zephaniah 3:17).

I believe God sings over us all the time, but especially while we're sleeping. I say that because I remember waking up with a song in my heart, I knew God had probably been singing that song over me all night. Oftentimes I would then take that song and sing it all through the day.

Another great song that was extremely comforting to me when I felt overwhelmed was a song written by Casting Crowns. The title is "*I Will Praise You in This Storm.*" I hope you will listen to it sometime. I know you will be blessed by its lyrics and message.

Can we still praise the God who gives and takes away when it's our children at stake? When everything we dreamed for them looks as though it's being taken away? Even their very lives? May we never forget that it was God who gave us our children, and, in reality, He has every right to take them away too. Even so, will we still trust that He knows best? Listen, my friend, singing songs of praise in your darkest hours may seem very simple, but it's extremely powerful. Again, the Devil and his demons aren't going to stay around very long when you start trusting God and singing songs with mountain moving faith written all over them. Words sung from the heart draw in the presence of God . . . and demons can't stand in His presence! *But you are holy, O you that inhabit the praises . . .* (Psalms 22:3 American KJV). Just as soon as you feel depressed, discouraged, or defeated, surrender your heart to God in song. Trust me, God knows this is a sacrifice of praise to Him from the depth of your weary soul, especially if it's the last thing you feel like doing. Offer it as a sacrifice of praise. Though your heart may be storm-battered and torn, remember to always praise Him.

Therefore, let us offer through Jesus a continual sacrifice of praise to God, proclaiming our allegiance to his name (Hebrews 13:15 NLT).

Oftentimes, as I sang through my darkest days, I thought God would step right in at any moment and the war would soon be over. But God's timing isn't ours. Therefore we march on by faith, believing the victory is ours, all the while serving Him with our whole heart. That's how we declare and proclaim our allegiance to His name.

Keep in mind, when you make declarations in songs to God, you are drawing the battle lines and letting Satan know where your allegiance lies. We must always be faithful to our Lord and Savior Jesus Christ, no matter the storm. I will praise you in the storm

His master replied, "Well done, good and faithful servant! . . . Come and share in your master's happiness!" (Matthew 25:21).

If you stay in the fight and don't give up, you too will share in your Master's happiness. What a wonderful and glorious day it will be when you hear Him say: *Well done, good and faithful servant!*

I know God is beaming with delight as He watches you go. I believe He is raising up super-victors in these last days, who have the same overcoming spirit as His Son Jesus Christ. As I have said before, He was the greatest example of an overcomer.

Don't let the Devil steal your victory. Keep your eyes on the Lord of the storm who says, "Come!" Stay focused and keep singing your victory song while you walk on the water with Jesus . . . even as the storm rages all around you! *Yes, we were made to do even greater things than these* (John 14:12).

"Come," he said. Then Peter got down out of the boat, walked on the water and came toward Jesus (Matthew 14:29).

14

First the Test—Then the Promotion!

Do not be afraid of what you are about to suffer. I tell you, the devil will put some of you in prison to test you, and you will suffer persecution . . . Be faithful, even to the point of death (Revelation 2:10).

Have you come to a place of brokenness, even to the point of death? Then you're at the perfect place to be used for God. My friend, when we get to this point of brokenness, the sanctification process is about over and we're almost ready to be of great use in the kingdom of God.

The LORD is close to the brokenhearted; he rescues those whose spirits are crushed. (Psalm 34:18 NLT).

As the Psalmist says, *the LORD is close . . . very close to the brokenhearted when they cry out to Him, and He listens to the godly person who does his will* (John 9:31). I saw this in my own life as the Lord encouraged me to start writing this book while still in my brokenness. We see this in all of His disciple's lives too: It was at this point of brokenness that they finally realized it wasn't about them, it was about Jesus and what God was calling them to do to impact His kingdom as servants of God. So, my friend, now that you have come to that place of brokenness too, ask yourself, "What is it that God is calling me to do for His kingdom?"

Start right there and begin to take deliberate steps in whatever direction God shows you. Keep pushing through until your life is being poured out for the glory of God; yes, let Him pour through you into the lives of others.

You see, brokenness brings you into sanctification and sanctification brings you into purification. Thus, glorification begins to take place in your life that is hidden in Christ. Then you will know that all the suffering was for the glory of God. When this process is completed, you will know it's time to *arise, shine, for your light has come, and the glory of the LORD rises upon you* (Isaiah 60:1).

Yes my friend, *The Lord rises upon you and his glory appears over you.* (Isaiah 60:2) He is the holy and glorious One, and He is making you holy so the people who are bound in darkness can see the glory of God in you and find hope.

See, darkness covers the earth and thick darkness is over the peoples, but the LORD rises upon you and his glory appears over you (Isaiah 60:2).

God pours out His love through pure, sanctified vessels. If you are broken right now, then begin to thank Him for your brokenness, because He is preparing you for what He has already prepared *for* you in the season or (Promised Land) up ahead. If members of your family are broken too, then let God have His way . . . don't run in and try to fix their lives. Pray for them to find the God of truth so the truth will set them free from their broken state too.

If you're in a harsh and difficult season right now, God has a very good reason for allowing you to go through this season or He wouldn't allow it at all. Any farmer will tell you how crucial it is to have an extremely cold winter season with at least two good hard freezes. Why would that be a good thing, you might ask? Because the bugs from the last season won't die unless there's a hard freeze. If the bugs don't die, then they will come back in the next season and eat the fruit that the farmers planted. My friend, this hard, harsh season that you are going through right now is a time when God is killing off the bugs that would eat the fruit of your next season. Trust Him and let Him have His way in your life, because if you don't, you will continually find yourself dealing with the same troublesome issues (or bugs) over and over again. Ask God, "What am I doing that keeps destroying my fruit?" When He identifies it, then ask Him to help let this thing die in your life.

Yes, I believe God is taking you and your prodigal through this season of extreme difficulty in order to kill off some things in your lives that would destroy what He has planned for all of you in the next season. Again, let God have His way and let those old bugs die as He reveals each one to you. This is what the sanctification process is all about! *Consider how far you have fallen! Repent and do the things you did at first.* (Revelation 2:5)

The truth is, we all have to come to this place of brokenness in order for the sanctification process to begin. This is how we die spiritually to ourselves. For some, it may take a prison sentence or jail time. For others it could mean starting all over again because of losing everything they own. Perhaps losing a loved one, or having their children or grandchildren taken away for a season. Nevertheless, whatever the Lord allows to happen in our lives, He will use it for our good if we will allow Him to take our time of brokenness and make it into something useful for His kingdom.

According to the Word of God, every season has a time and purpose for that season:

To every thing there is a season, and a time to every purpose under the heaven: a time to be born, and a time to die; a time to plant, and a time to pluck up that which is planted (Ecclesiastes 3:-12 KJV).

Yes, a time to die. Rock bottom is a great foundation to build from as God sees it, because He can help us start over again using His solid Rock of our salvation—Jesus Christ! Now, with Christ as our strong and firm foundation, He can drop His plumb line into our hearts and begin the building process once again; making us into what He originally designed us to be—sons and daughters of the living God! At this point, you're not balanced...you're leveled, by the hand of Almighty God!

Do not despise these small beginnings, for the LORD rejoices to see the work begin, to see the plumb line in Zerubbabel's hand. "... (Zechariah 4:10 NLT)

So the LORD stirred up the spirit of Zerubbabel (Haggai 1:14).

The truth is, from the day we were born, we were all originally designed to be warriors of the cross. Yet with our own freewill, we built our lives to suit ourselves and what we wanted instead. Nevertheless, now that we have come to the point of brokenness, God can stir us up and rebuild our lives to be all we never knew they could be. The hidden life in Christ now has a chance to start forming. Therefore if things are extremely painful right now, again I say, let Him have His way, my friend, and become all that He originally purposed you to be in this life. Your true purpose and new life is about to begin as you discover who you *really* are in Christ—broken bread and poured out wine, just as He was for the dying world!

This is my blood of the covenant, which is poured out for many for the forgiveness of sins (Matthew 26:28).

Jesus went through His seasons of testing while here on this earth, and now God is requiring the same thing from you before He will promote you to your next season.

Have you ever heard the saying, "Without a test, there can be no testimony?" The truth is, no one really enjoys a test of any kind. Even when they're well prepared, their emotions still run high because they don't know all that will be involved in the test, or how difficult it may be. And God forbid they barely studied for the test, or, worse yet, didn't study at all. That's when anxiety really takes over!

It's the same way with a spiritual test. God's Word prepares us for the spiritual tests that are sure to come our way. But what if we haven't been seriously studying God's Word? I think you know the answer to that question: we probably won't pass that test.

And since we don't know when these spiritual pop quizzes will come up, we need to stay studied up and prepared for whatever may come.

The Bible is filled with people who were given pop quizzes. Some failed their test, and we see the results of what happened in their lives afterward. Others were prepared and conquered the test and received their promotion. But the most famous and exciting stories are the ones where they didn't have a clue, but followed God's leading and ended up scoring an A-plus. You know the ones, where there was absolutely no way they could have done it without trusting God and stepping out in faith. Yes, He has all the answers to the test, we just need to seek Him for the answers.

Oh yeah, we all love to read the stories with incredible endings, but we can also learn a lot from seeing how that person handled the test. The truth is, their victory can become ours too if we follow the same God-given strategy in our own lives when we are tested, no matter what season we are in at the time.

In every story, there is a hero and a villain. In our lives, we know who that old antagonist is, the one who always tends to have a negative effect on our character. The truth is, that old, ancient serpent has been around even before there was time as we know it. If we will take the time to study the Bible, we will see that he uses the same old timeless tricks. Therefore if we learn his tricks, then we will have a better chance of passing the test when he tries one of them on us.

Do not be afraid of what you are about to suffer. I tell you, the Devil will put some of you in prison to test you, and you will suffer (Revelation 2:10).

Keep in mind as you read the verse above, it was written by the apostle John, one of Jesus' disciples and closest companions while He lived upon the earth. The main theme in this scripture is to trust God explicitly during your most difficult times of testing. Notice, this passage isn't saying *if* you are tested; it is letting you know you *will* be tested as a follower of Jesus Christ. Also, there *will* be suffering; however, if you pass the test, even if it costs you your life, God will reward you, either here on earth or on the other side of this life, in heaven. God always keeps His promises, and there is a great reward in store for you if you pass the test! We will talk more about these glorious rewards in the final chapter.

But for now, let's look at how we receive some of our rewards. We all know that the gift of eternal life was a free gift, which cost us absolutely nothing, right? The Word of God says, *For it is by grace you have been saved, through faith—and this is not from yourselves, it is the gift of God—not by works, so that no one can boast* (Ephesians 2:8-9). This scripture alone settles the matter.

It's because of the amazing grace of God and what Christ did on the cross that we are saved through faith in Jesus. This unbelievable gift was given to us because God loved us so much that He couldn't bear spending eternity without us. The last thing God wants is for us to be separated from His presence for all eternity. If you have trouble believing that, then think about what that gift cost Him: what He treasured most in all eternity—His one and only Son! Even though He knew He was giving up the treasure of His heart, He still went through with it, because He knew it was the only plan that would make our returning to Him possible. Therefore, He asked His only Son to come to earth and die a shameful criminal's death on a cross so that we could be united with Him throughout eternity. I don't know about you, but I believe God has every right to ask the same from any one of us.

Why should we be shielded from giving up our lives while here on this earth in order to do the Father's will? Think about it: Jesus did nothing wrong, yet He was accused of a crime. Not only that, He was convicted and sentenced to a criminal's death after basically being slaughtered before He got to the cross. Knowing that God the Father allowed His Son to suffer that kind of persecution shows me how dearly He loves His earthly children. Also, from reading the Scriptures, I believe the Lord Jesus would never require more of us than He was willing to give of Himself.

So why do we fall apart at the first grip of pain, and question God's love for us?

God never said it was always going to be easy. He has been completely honest with us from the beginning of the Bible to the very end in telling us that we live in a fallen and broken world—where there *will* be trouble.

Here on earth you will have many trials and sorrows. But take heart, because I have overcome the world (John 16:33 NLT).

Yes, salvation was offered to us freely, but we still have to live out our devotion to the Lord in a fallen world where the evil ones live and dwell among us. I have come to the conclusion, from reading the Scriptures, that God will allow the Devil to do certain things in our lives in order to strengthen our faith and our relationship with Him. We see this throughout the Bible as we look at many others who were completely innocent yet suffered greatly at the hands of the Devil and the evil people he used to do his bidding . . . Christ being one of the greatest sufferers of them all!

Although Jesus was the only completely blameless One, whom God sent as a sin offering to die for the sins of mankind and save our souls, He wasn't the first person who God loved dearly, yet allowed Satan to torment and cause incredible pain and suffering. Nor was Jesus the first to prove His complete devotion and allegiance to God by going through with his decision to surrender His will to the Father's will. No, many more God-fearing believers in both the Old and New Testament were required to pass the test of their faith—even unto death—before God promoted them to a place of honor. So the old excuse that Jesus was able to endure all these things because He was the Christ and empowered by the Holy Spirit doesn't give us an excuse to bow out. Let's face it: we have the same Holy Spirit living inside of us too right now. We need only to look at the lives of others who had a strong faith and love for their God, and see how they lived it out, even unto death if necessary. In the Old Testament, the Holy Spirit would come upon them and empower them to do great and mighty things.

Those people were normal men and women, just like us. Everyone who lived before the Spirit was poured out on the day of Pentecost didn't have the Holy Spirit (God) abiding in them like we do today.

The Bible says, *The Spirit of the LORD came powerfully upon him so that he tore the lion apart with his bare hands as he might have torn a young goat* (Judges 14:6). We can see from reading this scripture, and many more throughout the Word of God, that the Spirit of the Lord would come upon people and empower them to do great and mighty things in the Old Testament, but He didn't live inside of them before the Holy Spirit was poured out after Jesus' ascension into heaven.

Jesus said, *Very truly I tell you, whoever believes in me will do the works I have been doing, and they will do even greater things than these, because I am going to the Father* (John 14:12). My friend, if Jesus said that, as believers, we would do even greater things then Him, we must ask ourselves, "Why aren't we doing them?" Could our trials be an opportunity or a gateway to do even greater things for God while we suffer persecution? Jesus raised the dead, now because we have the same Holy Spirit, He's asking us to raise the dead too by prophesying to them the Word of the Lord. My friend, these are the greater things that Jesus was talking about!

Jesus warned us that, for His sake, we would suffer at the hands of the enemy.

Then you will be handed over to be persecuted and put to death, and you will be hated by all nations because of me (Matthew 24:9).

If the world hates you, keep in mind that it hated me first (John 15:18).

So it shouldn't come as a surprise to us when trials, tribulations, and false accusations come against us too. It seems like the confusion comes in when we feel like we did nothing to deserve our pain. That's understandable. However, have you ever thought that God may have allowed your pain to test your faith? Could it be that God was bragging on you, like many parents do about their children, and someone challenged God on your character and devotion to Him? That's what happened to Job. Job was like any true believer today: he was trying to live a life that was pleasing to God, and making sacrifices to keep his kids out of trouble.

Then God bragged to Satan about His good and faithful servant Job:

Then the Lord said to Satan, "Have you considered my servant Job? There is no one on earth like him; he is blameless and upright, a man who fears God and shuns evil" (Job 1:8).

That sounds like a good Christian person to me. I know several of those good folks.

Then Satan said to God, *Does Job fear God for nothing?. . . Have you not put a hedge around him and his household and everything he has? You have blessed the work of his hands, so that his flocks and herds are spread throughout the land. But now stretch out your hand and strike everything he has, and he will surely curse you to your face* (Job 1:9-11).

As we read on, we see that God the Father was so confident that Job would pass the test, He took Satan up on his challenge! Think about it. God had that much confidence in Job's character and devotion to Him. Believe me, God was counting on Job to prove the Devil wrong and bring honor to His holy name. Therefore God *allowed* the Devil to test Job. Again, if God is allowing suffering in your life right now, let Him have His way and, while doing so, to the best of your ability, trust His holy character and bring honor to His name.

The Word of God also says, *My people are destroyed from lack of knowledge* (Hosea 4:6). This is no time to be ignorant to the ways of your enemy. Know the Word of God and you will know how the enemy operates, and, more importantly, you will know how to defeat him!

Our God is far more loving and caring than the most loving parent that ever lived, and He is always on our side, so we need to trust Him explicitly, especially when we don't understand what's going on in our lives. Look at Job. He didn't have a clue why he was being targeted for destruction. Although, as the Bible says, he was the most righteous man in the land. Yet Satan was wiping him out and destroying everything he held most precious in this world, and that included his kids. And God was allowing it! But Job never gave up on God. Why? Because He had come to know and trust his loving God in a very personal way. He trusted God's character more than the pain of his personal circumstances. Do you know Him like that?

Job 38:1, says, *Then the Lord spoke to Job out of the storm.* When God spoke to Job right in the middle of his storm, he not only recognized God's voice, but God's words immediately brought him to a place of complete surrender and brokenness. After that, Job's confidence and trust in God became even greater, as he rose up and got on through his valley. The Word of God tells us that Job's latter days are one of the greatest testimonies of seeing *the goodness of the Lord in the land of the living:*

I will remain confident of this: I will see the goodness of the LORD in the land of the living (Psalm 27:13).

And that, my friend, is how we keep advancing against the evil one—by remaining confident in God and trusting His holy character as we surrender to His will.

As we look at Job's story, we first see where his soul was tested (will, mind and emotions). Interestingly enough, Satan went for his kids and livelihood first. The next area of testing was his body (pain and physical suffering). Then finally, his spirit was tested (wisdom, communion and conscience). You might say Job went through all three dark nights of testing, since we are basically made up of three parts: body, soul, and spirit.

I will explain the three dark nights in greater detail a little later in this chapter. But for now, I want to challenge you to question your own heart and ask yourself: If God looked down from heaven and pointed me out to the Devil, bragging on me for being such a righteous, upright person, would I pass the test that Job was given and honor God by proving the Devil wrong? Keep in mind, Job did not have the Holy Spirit living inside of him as you do; and no where do we read that the Spirit of God came upon him and empowered him either. No, God simply said, *He is blameless and upright, a man who fears God and shuns evil* (Job 1:8).

As I said before, that sounds like many normal everyday Christians to me, how about you?

I must admit, I never wanted to have God's finger pointing me out to Satan, let alone have my family given over to him. However, I believe that while we live in this fallen world, God counts on us in the same way He counted on Job. God wants us to pass the test too, during our most difficult trying times, and prove the Devil wrong. Could it be that we, like Job, are being put to the test when, out of nowhere, disaster strikes with one blow after the other?

As we read Job's story, we see that's what happened to him. And what was the first thing Satan went after? Job's children. Satan knows our weakness: those we love the most here on this earth—our kids! And why wouldn't we? They are flesh of our flesh and a gift to us from God. Even our adopted children have the same attachment to our soul because of the bond we share with them as special gifts from God. I can honestly say, there is absolutely no difference in my heart between my adopted granddaughter and my two natural grandsons.

The point is, if we see God allowing Satan to test His children in the Bible with the even-unto-death test, why would we think we're immune from the same test? I mean, He's the same God, right?

For I am the LORD, I change not (Malachi 3:6 KJV).

Also, we read in Hebrews 13:8, *Jesus Christ is the same yesterday and today and forever* (KJV).

From reading His Word, I've come to believe that we are not immune, and He still tests us today, sometimes allowing the Devil to be used if necessary. If this is so, then we must ask ourselves the question, *why* is He allowing us to be tested?

The answer is simple: to see if our devotion to Him is firmly grounded, so that He may use us to help advance His Kingdom. God won't promote us to the next level of leadership if we can't pass even the simplest test of faith first!

Now the truth is, God already knows where we are in our devotion to Him, but *we* only know it when we pass the test. When our faith is tested, we grow. The more difficult the test, the more we grow. We see this same concept over and over again throughout the Bible, where God's people are tested right before He promotes them. The trials and severity of test may vary, but the main theme is always the same: *first comes the test, then comes the promotion!*

And let us not forget, according to His Word, God not only promotes us when we pass the test, He rewards us for our faithfulness too! Our promotion is like the trophy God gives us for winning the race. And once we've proven ourselves to be super-victors, God expects us to help train others to be exceptional runners in this race called life too!

For this reason, I believe God sometimes allows pain and suffering to come into our lives, even when we've done nothing to cause it. Our loving God has a purpose and plan for everything He allows to happen in our lives. He doesn't make random choices and then hope it all comes out okay in the end, like most of us do. No—our God has a plan for our lives, and everything He allows to happen to us has purpose and meaning. He says, *For I know the plans I have for you . . . plans to prosper you and not harm you, plans to give you hope and a future* (Jeremiah 29:11).

There you have it! Everything God allows to happen in our lives has destiny written all over it. Everything happens for our good—even what the Devil intended for evil.

You intended to harm me, but God intended it for good to accomplish what is now being done, the saving of many lives (Genesis 50:20).

What was the ultimate purpose behind all of our suffering? *The saving of many lives.*

The dying world needs to hear and see our testimony. We are tested in order that others may find hope through our suffering, and that goes for our Christian brothers and sisters too. Unfortunately, most people—myself included—don't always understand the why behind the what. In other words, *why* would our loving God allow so much suffering and destruction to go on in our lives and *what* good could possibly come out of it? The why is the hardest question to answer, and we need not spend too much time lingering there for an answer, because Satan will gladly give you his thoughts on the matter! There could be a multiplicity of reasons why God has allowed our suffering, but we know from reading His Word, He will use it for our good if we will trust Him. Yes, He knows the plans He has for us, and they are for our good and our future. Therefore we don't need to always know the why or the what. We just need to trust Him to be the wise and all-knowing God He is and to believe that He has a good plan for our lives, no matter what we're going through here on this earth right now.

Let's face it: All of our sin is really a product of not trusting God! We worry because we don't trust God to meet our needs or protect our children. Worrying says, *I can't trust God to answer my prayers or meet my needs.* For example, in order to have peace of mind financially, we save our money, but we never feel like it's enough, even when it's a great sum of money. Not that having a savings account is wrong, but when we have it and keep growing it because we don't trust God to provide for our needs, then something is wrong with our trust in God. He wants us to trust Him in every area of our lives, especially when it comes to answering our prayers and meeting our needs.

I have been young, and now am old; yet I have not seen the righteous forsaken, nor his children begging for bread. (Psalm 37:25 WEB).

I do know from reading the Scriptures, and the times I tried this in my own life; we can bring severe punishment upon ourselves when we willfully fail to trust God to come through for us and take matters in our own hands. Or, worse yet, when we willfully give up on serving Him altogether. Willful disobedience leads to a dangerous path of destruction and straight into the Devil's den. And trust me, God has nothing to do with that. We choose that path all on our own. I would say, much of what we suffer in life comes from our own willful sin and lack of self-discipline to trust God and wait on Him. Again, I know this to be true in my own life. I've gotten myself into most of my troubles by taking matters into my own hands and doing it my own way instead of His way. Afterward, I would pray for God's forgiveness and ask Him to get me out of the trouble I'm in . . . Does that sound familiar?

Many times He has rescued me from my own self-imposed trap, however, there have been times when God let me learn from my own disobedience and I suffered the consequences. Or you might say, He used it to kill off some bugs that needed to die. I soon learned to repent from the depths of my heart and stop doing those destructive things that certainly didn't bring glory to His name. I knew in my heart that my suffering was a result of not trusting God, and, at that time, I felt as though I deserved all the suffering I was getting. Believe me, correction is a good thing. There are times we all need to be corrected; if not we would destroy the fruit God has for us in the next season. If God is disciplining you or your prodigal child right now, then I would encourage you to take that as a good sign. A sign that both of you belong to God, *because the Lord disciplines the one he loves, and chastens everyone he accepts as his son* (Hebrews 12:6).

As we continue to look at some of the reasons God allows suffering and trials to come our way, we can't overlook unrepented sin. We see throughout the Bible where God allowed trouble to come into people's lives because of unrepented sin, especially those He called to a specific purpose.

The Word of God tells us, *all have sinned and fall short of the glory of God, and all are justified freely by his grace through the redemption that came by Christ Jesus* (Romans 3:23-24).

As we read the story of Adam and Eve, we see what their *real* sin was—not trusting God. After God gave them strict specific instructions about what was allowed and what wasn't, they still believed the Devil's lies, instead of trusting God's character and what He told them. Satan basically twisted God's words and, in essence, said to Eve, *God is holding out on you and not telling you everything. There is so much more you're missing out on!*

Isn't that the same old lie he tells our children when he lures them into the world? They are deceived by their own lust of wanting more, just like Eve was, and, by doing so, they're led into the world and away from God's place of safety. Nevertheless, the fact still remains, we all went that way because we didn't trust God's words to be true. And the Word of God says, *people are without excuse.* (Romans 1:20) Why? *For since the creation of the world God's invisible qualities---his eternal power and divine nature---have been clearly seen, being understood from what has been made, so that people are without excuse.* Also, if that wasn't enough, the warnings are all written out in the Ten Commandments. It's pretty simple. Yes, all of our sinful actions can be summed up by the same original sin—the sin of not trusting God! The truth is, God's rules were written for our good. He's not trying to keep us from something good, but from something bad that will destroy our lives if we don't follow His commands. Jesus came to fulfil the laws of God and bring grace. Now Jesus is saying we are to: *Love the Lord your God with all your heart and with all your soul and with all your mind and with all your strength. The second is this: 'Love your neighbor as yourself. There is no commandments greater then these."*

Unfortunately, because of the sinful nature we inherited from Adam and Eve due to their disobedience, we are all going to fail the test from time to time and be deceived by the evil one. But thanks be to God the Father, through His Son Jesus Christ, we now are justified by grace (or made sinless), through our profession of faith in Him as our Lord and Savior. Our precious Lord Jesus suffered and endured the cross because of someone else's sin . . . *ours!* He didn't do anything to deserve that suffering and pain, but because He loved us so much, He shed His own blood to cover all our sins. We are God's children. The very ones who willfully sinned against His Holy Word and caused all of Christ's suffering.

I can understand God's depth of love in my own limited way because of how much I love my own children. I would lay down my life for any one of them. Also, I never left them or forsook them during their times of great need. No, to the best of my ability, with God's wise counsel, I encouraged them and helped them back into a place of wholeness. Sometimes, even speaking correction that they really didn't want to hear. Isn't that what Jesus did for us? Just because both of my sons' disobedience caused all of us great, undeserved suffering, we didn't abandon them. However, there were times when God gave us strict instructions to let them suffer for a while so they could learn from their disobedience. We knew this was a time of correction in their lives, so we allowed God to have His way. We believed it was a correction that was needed in order to keep them from destruction. As I previously explained, that's why we left our eldest son in jail the second time.

Unfortunately, there are times we won't learn the lesson God is trying to teach us unless we suffer the consequences of our actions for a while. The truth is, there are certain requirements that our loving Father demands of His children, and *all* of them are to keep us safe. If those requirements aren't heeded, the Father will use whatever resources necessary to teach us a lesson we will never forget—just to protect us from the enemy's destructive plans!

As a parent, wouldn't you agree that you're always looking for the best and most reasonable way to get your kids to heed the warnings you give them, in order to keep them safe? And while they were young, didn't you have safe boundaries set up to reinforce their safety? Of course you did! Well, our loving Father does too.

God is not out of line when he corrects and disciplines us, or even when He allows us to be tested. And we should know Him well enough by now that we don't always need to know the *why* behind the *what*! As I said before, if God is allowing it, then let Him have His way; somehow, it's part of His good master plan for us!

I don't know about you, but as for me, I can't seem to get by with anything! There are things I see other Christians doing that I know are against God's Word, but it seems as though God allows it for a season without correcting them. And I remember when God used to give me the same measure of grace in my early walk with Him too. But now that I'm more mature in my walk, I know why God won't let me get by with these same sins anymore. The answer goes all the way back to the beginning of my walk with Him, when I prayed this prayer: *Lord, I want everything you have for me in my life! I know you have so much more for me, and I want it all!*

After 39 years of following Him as closely as I possibly could, I understand that more will be required of me than others who may not have prayed that same prayer.

From everyone who has been given much, much will be demanded; and from the one who has been entrusted with much, much more will be asked (Luke 12:48).

Is this you too right now? Have you asked God to give you a closer walk with Him? If so, *much will be demanded* from you too. From reading this scripture, I know I'm responsible before God to live a life that mirrors His ways before men. I'm not a baby Christian, I'm a mature believer who has been given much, spiritually speaking; therefore, He requires and expects more from me than from a new believer. I'm not going to get by with things others may get by with, because, as His adult daughter, I should be a reflection of Him in every area of my life now. My God is excellent and perfect in all His ways, therefore, as his daughter, He requires excellence from me as well. We know God's standard of excellence because He tells us in His Word, *Be perfect, therefore, as your heavenly Father is perfect* (Matthew 5:48). Thank God we are made perfect through Christ and His righteousness or we would never be able to accomplish His standard of perfection. Nevertheless, God still requires righteous living from His children.

I'm reminded of when Joyce Meyer was talking about this same subject in one of her wonderful teachings. She shared a story where she was complaining to God about what others could get by with and yet still be blessed by God anyway. Then she asked Him why she couldn't get by with those things without being corrected. And this is what He told her:

"Joyce, you have asked for a lot. Do you want it or not?"

Well, that pretty much says it all.

I don't know about you, but I'm willing to do some suffering if it means getting the *much more* God has for me! For one thing, at the very least, I believe I owe Him that much for all He has done for me. I don't want to be like one of those ungrateful lepers who didn't even come back and say thank you to Jesus after He healed them. No, I want to live a life that says thank you every time I do what is right. Yes, every time I lead someone into the saving knowledge of who He is. And, most importantly, every time Satan challenges God on my devotion to Him. When Satan says, *She won't pass that test! Let me go after her children and tear their lives apart, then she will curse You to Your face!* I want the response of my action and words to be, *No, I won't; not for anything this world has to offer. I won't curse my God and I won't fail this test or bow to you either!"*

One thing I know by now, with Jesus at my right hand, I really *can* do all things!

I can do all things through Christ which strengthens me (Philippians 4:13 KJV).

Christ says I can do all things, therefore I know I can pass that test with Him at my right hand—even if Satan turns up the heat to an unbearable temperature. You know why? Because I have set my mind ahead of time, and I'm determined to be the one leper who came back and fell at Jesus' feet, thanking him for what he did for me on the cross:

He fell to the ground at Jesus' feet, thanking him for what he had done (Luke 17:16 NLT).

I can't wonder where the other nine are and spend time justifying my lack of gratefulness by comparing myself to them. I just need to decide if I'm going to live a life that brings honor to God or not. I want to honor the One who passed the greatest test of all and died for a sinful, yet grateful, leper like me.

How about you?

I believe it's time we decide to grow up spiritually and stop trying to justify our sin by comparing ourselves to others and start being what God called all of us to be—sons of God! Sons of God are loyal knights, warriors of God, who won't back down, fail, or disappoint Him, even if it costs them their lives.

This was a choice I had to make early on as I walked through the darkest days of my life, when my treasured dreams and hopes were being dashed on the rocks below and trampled underfoot by the evil one. Trust me when I say, nothing made sense to me at that time. And, worse yet, God didn't give me any explanations or answers before He simply said, *Live in the victory. Don't wait until you have the victory to rejoice, but rejoice now knowing it is yours!*

Nonetheless, I understood clearly what those words meant: God was letting me know He already saw the beginning and the end of my journey through this dark valley. He was simply asking me to trust Him with what I held most precious on this earth—all without knowing why He was allowing it to happen. He was basically asking me, *Can you believe what I am saying to you right now and trust me to work everything together for good, even without an explanation?*

In that moment, when He said those words to me, I didn't have all the answers. But He was letting me know He did!

I can honestly say, I learned many things throughout this journey, but the most important thing I learned was this: it's not a matter of whether you get what you want or even if you win the war; it's a matter of allowing God to have His way, no matter what the cost, and letting Him reign in your life!

***

The most exciting and rewarding part of going through all I've gone through is the new level of faith I have in Him. Throughout my difficult journey, God proved His faithfulness to me over and over again. So much so that I have given Him a nickname: The King of Cool!

I have found that God always does things in the coolest and most unbelievable ways. It's amazing to watch how He works something out. When we surrender to God and allow Him to get actively involved in a situation, it never comes out in the end like you thought it would; it always comes out in a way that blows your mind!

The Lord's unfailing love surrounds the one who trusts in him (Psalm 32:10).

Yes, it was in the valley of brokenness and testing that I came to know and trust my Lord and Savior in a whole new way. Now I thank Him for my many experiences—the glorious ones and the dreadful ones that brought me to a place of brokenness—because they have caused me to fall completely in love with Him. I freely submit my will over to His because I know I can trust Him. I say with complete confidence, *Thy will be done, O Lord, on earth as it is in heaven; let what brings you glory and joy be done in my life.* So don't dread the valley, my friend, because in that valley, He is opening up rivers of refreshing waters that will lead you to your real life that was hidden in Christ.

For you died to this life, and your real life is hidden with Christ in God (Colossians 3:3 NLT).

You see, because of my journey through the dark valley, *God* has become my earthly and heavenly treasure—not money, houses, cars, or my husband, not even my children and grandchildren. No, none of these things compare to the matchless treasure I have found in Him. He has completely transfigured my way of looking at things, and the way my sons look at things too now.

I was talking to my oldest son recently about our difficult time in the valley. And you know what he said? He said, "I don't regret going to prison. I know God used it to change me into the man I am today."

I'm so thankful for my journey through the dark valley too, because, like my son, it was in the dark valley that I finally found the true, incomparable treasure of being one with my Father God, Lord and Savior Jesus Christ, and Holy Spirit. That time in prison with my son actually made me the woman I am today. This oneness that I have now will always be my greatest reward in this life. Not to mention, this was Jesus' heart's desire for all of us when He prayed this prayer:

My prayer is not for them alone. I pray also for those who will believe in me through their message, that all of them may be one, Father, just as you are in me and I am in you. May they also be in us so that the world may believe that you have sent me. I have given them the glory that you gave me, that they may be one as we are one—I in them and you in me— so that they may be brought to complete unity (John 17:20-23).

The incomparable treasure that was matchless and precious to Jesus was for us to know our heavenly Father in such a personal and intimate way as He did.

Now, my friend, I ask you these question: Could this be the road marked with suffering that Paul was talking about? Could this be what's happening in your life right now?

Resist him, standing firm in the faith, because you know that the family of believers throughout the world is undergoing the same kind of sufferings. And the God of all grace, who called you to his eternal glory in Christ, after you have suffered a little while, will himself restore you and make you strong, firm and steadfast. To him be the power for ever and ever. Amen (1 Peter 5:9-11).

Does God have you on this broken road for a purpose and destiny that can only be revealed by walking down it? If so, remember, Jesus said, *If any man will come after me, let him deny himself, and take up his cross, and follow me* (Matthew 16:24 KJV). It may be that this is your cross to carry, and Satan is saying, *She will never make it!* But Jesus reaches out with His nail-scarred hand and says, *Follow me. I'll help you!*

Very truly I tell you, whoever believes in me will do the works I have been doing, and they will do even greater things than these (John 14:12).

My friend, it's time to let go of worry, fear, and doubt; take hold of your Savior's nail-scarred hand—which bears the evidence of an overcomer—and let Him show us how an overcomer can do even greater things. Oswald Chambers understood the concept of suffering in this world in order to glorify God and have fellowship with His Son. He wrote in *My Utmost for His Highest* that through our heartbreaks, God opens doors that lead to fellowship with Jesus, and that through that fellowship, Jesus hopes to share in the burden of our yoke as we join forces with Him.

The LORD is with me like a mighty warrior; so my persecutors will stumble and not prevail (Jeremiah 20:11).

Again I say, it's time for the redeemed of the earth to join forces with the Mighty Warrior of heaven and fight with Him! If you will fight for your loved ones, I promise you God will come along beside you and fight with you! I can truly say from my own experience, God is faithful through every battle; His unfailing love will surround you and protect you as you trust Him.

As they pass through the Valley of Baka, they make it a place of springs; the autumn rains also cover it with pools. They go from strength to strength, till each appears before God in Zion (Psalms 84:6-7).

Little did we know, as we stood at the gates of sorrow and suffering, that those autumn rains would someday start pouring out, bringing us to places of refreshing pools and springs, where living water flowed! Keep in mind, the Valley of Baka, according to the Bible, was an evil place. Does that sound like the valley you're in right now? The question is, what will you turn your Valley of Baka into? Will you make it a place of refreshing springs for others to drink from, as those in this scripture did? Or will those streams become bitter because of your unwillingness to let the Valley of Baka transfigure you into the person God intended you to be?

And we know that in all things God works for the good of those who love him, who have been called according to his purpose (Romans 8:28).

In all things, including extremely difficult, heart-crushing things, God is still working all things together for our good. Every battle was designed to take us from strength to strength, and prepare us to appear before the God of Zion! As we can see from reading these two scriptures, there is a very important reason why God allows bad things to happen in our lives, even things that seem unfair or unjustified. Again, we see the why in the last verse of Romans 8:28 it says, *those who have been called according to his purpose*. Those who have been called for whose purpose? God's purpose, and it probably won't look like what you thought or intended it to look like either.

With that being said, do you believe that you have been called by God for a specific purpose? If so, His main goal is to get you to that place, where you can fulfill the purpose and call He has destined for you. The big question is, are you willing to let Him take control and fulfill His purpose instead of yours? If so, you will need to follow the Holy Spirit's leading very carefully, as He navigates you through this valley and into Father God's purpose for your life.

You see, the Holy Spirit is like our inner GPS system: when we get on the wrong road, we see Him "recalculating." It can be frustrating, and we seem to waste a lot of time on the wrong road, not getting to where we want to go. But God knows the right road and He's trying to get us back on it! That goes for our children too. Some of the detours they take seem to them at the time like a good idea. However, these detours can be painfully long and troublesome, not only for them, but for everyone who is traveling with them. And usually they cause us to stay lost much longer on those back roads than we intended. But God is faithful to recalculate our route on that road of suffering, and, in due time, He will navigate all of us back to the road that leads to our destiny and intended purpose.

I find it fascinating that no matter what wrong road we may be on, God has a way of teaching us something while we're there—something that will be useful for others—all the while getting us turned around to the right road. I would venture to say, this is what He is doing in your prodigal child's life too. God never gives up on us, He just keeps turning us around until we get on the right road!

Yes, God is using this time of testing in the valley to *restore you and make you strong, firm and steadfast* (1 Peter 5:10). He is strengthening and perfecting our faith in order to root us firmly in Him. God is using this time in the valley to train up a knight for the kingdom of God . . . a warrior of the faith.

Can you, too, see more clearly now, after reading this book, what God is up to in your prodigal child's life? And not only in their life, but yours as well? I'm not sure how far you are into your journey at this point, but I hope you are encouraged to keep moving forward by faith, now that you have a better idea of what the Father is up to. He is strengthening you and your prodigal child for an assignment He had planned all along. God knows what He's doing, and He knows what He has planned for us up ahead too. I believe it is during this time that He is preparing us for what He already has prepared for us. Yes, our destiny, is just sitting there waiting on us to arrive and take hold of it!

This is what the Apostle Paul was talking about when he said: *Not that I have already obtained all this, or have already arrived at my goal, but I press on to take hold of that for which Christ Jesus took hold of me* (Philippians 3:12).

Have you taken hold of the purpose for which Christ took hold of you? If so, then you have to get on through God's warrior training camp to be prepare for His intended purpose. He has a surprise and reward for you up ahead, all right—*if* you don't give up or quit during His boot camp training, that is.

During your time in God's boot camp, much will be required of you, including determined perseverance, which produces godly character. Godly character is extremely important because, without it, your witness will have no power. However, I must warn you: many don't pass God's training camp because they don't want to meet the requirements that God asks of them . . . the requirements to become sons of God. He requires from you the same thing He required from many other giants of the faith, including Job, David, Abraham, and His Son.

Remember the three dark nights that I talked about at the beginning of this chapter? Well, get ready to face each of these dark nights while in God's boot camp, or, I should say, *your dark valley*. Your flesh will be crucified, along with your soul and spirit, as you learn to die to the things that are not of God. God's training camp is meant to transform us into sons of God as we pass one test after the other. You might say, He takes us from glory to glory until we reach the place where He can trust us to handle the things of His kingdom properly. Promotion to the next level will only come as we pass those tests of faith along the dark valley road of suffering. The good news is, we never really fail; we just keep taking the same test over again until we pass. Unfortunately, each time we fail, it takes longer to get to a place of usefulness for God.

Now that you've been given a glimpse of what you'll face while in God's training camp, and why you are there in the first place, I would encourage you to watch a video by John Paul Jackson. His teaching called "*The Mystery of The Three Dark Nights*" resonated in my spirit when I heard it. It gave me incredible insight and understanding that I only seemed to have pieces of before I heard it. I believe it will bring clarity to what you may be struggling with too.

After listening to this thought-provoking teaching, I realized I had gone through all three of these dark nights along with my husband and two sons. Although all of us are still working out some of the details in this sanctification process, I know God is faithful and He will complete the good work He started in all of us.

I am sure of this, that he who started a good work in you will carry it on to completion until the day of Christ Jesus (Philippians 1:6 CSB).

It's amazing where children will take you. But when you love someone, there's no separating the two. Where they go, you go—even if it's off to prison! Even so, we didn't come out of the dark evil valley the same way we went in. Oh no, we are forever changed. As I think about where and what my children brought me through, I'm reminded that God's children's sin took Him to the cross to die. I guess you could say, in a way, my children took me there too.

As you follow John Paul Jackson's teaching on the three dark nights, I want you to compare your own journey through the dark valley, as I did. You may have just started your journey, or perhaps you are somewhere in the middle or even closer than you think to the end. But wherever you are at right now, this teaching will give you great insight into what lies ahead for you. It will also help prepare you for what God will require of you too. I wish I would have known about it early on in my journey.

Nevertheless, as I close out this chapter, I want to share with you my greatest take away from this time of brokenness and sanctification. I would have to say it was when I finally decided to surrender my will to God's will, not only for my own life, but for both of my son's lives as well. You see, I thought I needed to hold on to my dreams for them, but I was wrong. It wasn't until I let go of my dreams and my will for their lives and completely released them to God's will and plans that I saw something unfolding in their lives that went beyond anything I could ever have dreamed for them. As I said before, that was when real, rapid change started to accelerate in all of our lives. Yes, when I finally laid my two Isaacs down on God's sacrificial altar of grace and mercy, I was free!

You know why? Satan didn't have anything to hold over me anymore. I had completely released them to my Almighty God and all my fears of what might happen were gone. God was holding on to their hands now, and I didn't have to figure it all out any more. I just expected God to lead them through their dark valley and do great things in their lives.

And He did!

Yes, without a doubt, I'd have to say the most valuable lesson I learned through every season of testing was to trust God completely.

And that, my friend, is how wars are won!

Once that decision is made, the war is over and we soon find ourselves living in a whole new place . . . *the victor's circle!*

15

The Victor's Crown

Be faithful, even to the point of death, and I will give you life as your victor's crown (Revelation 2:10).

One beautiful, sunny spring morning in 2013, as I sat under an oak tree in my back yard praying, the Lord spoke to me. He said, "Daughter, you have won. You have overcome by the word of your testimony and the blood of the Lamb. You are standing in the victor's circle and you are wearing the victor's crown!"

In the morning, Lord, you hear my voice; in the morning I lay my requests before you and wait expectantly (Psalm 5:3).

In the thrill of that moment, I was completely overwhelmed with His presence and fullness of joy at what I'd heard my Lord say. The psalmist said, *Shouts of joy and victory resound in the tents of the righteous* (Psalm 118:15). This scripture describes perfectly what went on that morning in my back yard! Yes, He was letting me know the war was over; I had finally defeated my enemy and won the war!

That day, the final victory was declared in our favor. What a thrilling moment of rejoicing that was!

Rejoice in the Lord always. I will say it again: Rejoice! (Philippians 4:4).

At this time, I was in the tenth year of my long journey through the dark valley. Throughout my pilgrimage, I never stopped believing and living in a state of expectancy. I knew in my heart that I had been faithful to my Lord as I fought one battle after another, and I felt in my spirit it wouldn't be much longer before the victory was declared in our favor.

As I sat before the Lord that morning, slowly meditating over every amazing word He had just spoken to me, a thought ran through my mind: *What does the victor's crown look like?* I had my iPhone with me, so I decided to be all spiritual and . . . Google it.

When the photo popped up on my screen, I was shocked. It was a crown of thorns like Jesus wore. Oh my goodness! I guess I'd never thought too much about this particular crown until then. I knew Jesus was made to wear the crown of thorns as a way of publicly humiliating Him. That's just how Satan and his brood of vipers operate: they want all of us to look like a bunch of fools so they can exalt themselves and their agenda.

Oh yes, Satan was gloating over what he thought was his greatest victory, by mocking and humiliating Jesus, making a public spectacle of Him. Nonetheless, Jesus didn't let it detour Him from what He'd come to do—defeat Satan and take back the keys of death and hell.

I am the Living One; I was dead, and now look, I am alive for ever and ever! And I hold the keys of death and Hades (Revelation 1:18).

Little did old Satan know, as he sat there robbing Jesus of His dignity and gloating over what he thought was going to be his finest hour, that God had a hidden plan that would overthrow his kingdom of darkness once and for all! Just when he thought he had it all figured out, in reality, he was about to seal his own fate, by killing the Son of God. Oh yes, what he thought would be his ultimate victory became his own final demise. Satan's evil plan actually brought forth his own kingdom's destruction. And I'm sure he didn't realize it until he heard Jesus' final words on the cross, as he took his last breath and died for the sins of all mankind: *It is finished* (John 19:30).

Do not gloat over me, my enemy! Though I have fallen, I will rise. Though I sit in darkness, the LORD will be my light (Micah 7:8).

Now who looks like the fool?

Our Lord and victorious Savior Jesus Christ overcame every devious, demonic test in Satan's evil scheming plot against Him and carried out the perfect battle plan and strategy God had given Him. Satan didn't have the battle plan figured out, that's for sure, or he would have never crucified the Son of God and sealed his own eternal fate.

While trying his best to disgrace and humiliate me in every way imaginable, Satan was relentless in his attempt to rob me of my dignity too. Again, that's just the way he operates. It wasn't out of the question, since he'd done the same thing to my Lord and Savior. Nevertheless, even after years of studying and teaching the Word of God, I had never before made the correlation between the crown of thorns and a victor's crown.

As I looked at the picture, I thought, *I'm not worthy to wear that same crown.* What am I thinking? But I couldn't stop meditating on this amazing crown and the honor it was to share in His suffering.

Paul said, *And since we are his children, we are his heirs. In fact, together with Christ we are heirs of God's glory. But if we are to share his glory, we must also share his suffering.* (Romans 8:17 NLT).

Sharing in His suffering . . . this wasn't something I'd ever thought much about either before going through my dark journey. But, it made perfect sense now. As I looked back over the valley road behind me, I saw fragments of the same old evil plots the enemy used on Jesus being played out on me and my family. Oh yes, the Devil intended to bring shame and disgrace to our Lord and Savior, but what He did brought incredible glory, honor, praise, and rejoicing instead! Again, I believe that's why God told me from the beginning of the journey to rejoice now, knowing the victory was mine. He saw the evil plot of the enemy, and He also saw our victory too! God was *declaring the end from the beginning, and from ancient times the things that are not yet done, saying, My counsel shall stand, and I will do all my pleasure* (Isaiah 46:10 KJV).

We see this clearly as we look at Jesus' circumstances, not only did God reverse the enemy's plot against our Savior, God gave Him the final victory over Satan once and for all! Through this magnificent victory, Jesus gave the same blessed inheritance of everlasting life to whosoever acknowledges Him as Lord and Savior and asks forgiveness of their sins.

No one was more surprised than the evil deceiver Satan when the crown of thorns he'd used to mock and disgrace Jesus with was transfigured into the victor's crown that now identifies Him as the victorious overcoming Son of God!

The forever Super Victor over the forever loser, Satan.

God said, *I will do all my pleasure.* I believe God was laughing at the evil one's futile attempts, knowing that one day soon He would sit with His victorious Son again in heaven. I also believe when we see Jesus, He will be wearing that crown along with all the other crowns mentioned in the Bible.

But I bet that one is His personal favorite!

As I continued to think about that crown, I imagined what His new transfigured crown must look like. I imagined it made of solid gold, filled with stunning, brightly colored precious stones. I pictured every thorn covered in tiny, brilliant gems, each one representing the souls of those He redeemed on the cross the day He died, when he wore what Satan intended to be a mocking joke. But the Word of God says, *Do not be deceived: God cannot be mocked* (Galatians 6:7).

We won't be mocked either as we spend eternity wearing our promised crowns. We read in God's Word that five precious crowns will be given to the people of God who live an upright life before Him while here on this earth. They are known as the five heavenly crowns: the crown of righteousness, the crown of life, the crown of glory, the crown of exultation, and, finally, the victor's crown. They are the incorruptible crowns that Christian believers will receive after the Last Judgment.

The crown of life is spoken of in James 1:12:

Blessed is the one who perseveres under trial because, having stood the test, that person will receive the crown of life that the Lord has promised to those who love him.

Interestingly, one day, while reading the Word, I noticed that our crowns can be taken from us too. Jesus said, *I am coming soon. Hold on to what you have, so that no one will take your crown. The one who is victorious I will make a pillar in the temple of my God* (Revelation 3:11,12).

We all know by now who that thief is, the one who wants to steal our crowns. I believe that's why God encourages us throughout His Word to never give up: *Let us not become weary in doing good, for at the proper time we will reap a harvest if we do not give up* (Galatians 6:9). Also, Jesus said, *Look, I am coming soon! My reward is with me, and I will give to each person according to what they have done* (Revelation 22:12). Throughout God's Word, we see how God richly blessed those who passed the test and overcame the enemy's evil plots. Yes, those who persevere and overcome the powers of hell will receive a crown that will be worn in heaven forever. What an honor! Our Lord's greatest desire is: *to bestow on them a crown of beauty instead of ashes...* (Isaiah 61:3)

Hold on to what you have, so that no one will take your crown (Revelation 3:11). From reading this scripture, it sounds like we just could be wearing this crown already (spiritually speaking.) I mean, Jesus did say to me that day while under the tree: *You are wearing the victor's crown.*

Now just bear with me for a minute, because I can't help but wonder: could it be that we are given our crowns as we overcome here on the earth? If so, can these crowns be seen in the spirit realm? Whether this is so or not, I'm not sure. Nevertheless, whenever the Devil tries to tear down my dignity and identity in Christ, I just reach up and adjust my crown! It's a great reminder of whose I am, and what family I belong to—God's royal family.

My friend, on days when the enemy tries to get you to question your identity in Christ and who you are in Him, just reach up and adjust your crown too!

According to the Word of God in Revelation 4, the twenty-four elders fall down and worship God, then lay their crowns before the throne. One day we will lay our crowns at His throne too and say with the elders: *You are worthy, our Lord and God, to receive glory and honor and power* (Revelation 4:11). I can't wait to lay mine down before Him and bow to the King of Kings and the Lord of Lords! But first, I want to fill it with as many gemstones of souls and good deeds as I can. I want to see His face beam with delight on that day when this grateful leper says, "Thank You," as I lay my victor's crown down at His feet.

Yes, that will be a glorious day indeed. But, in the meantime, another glorious day has arrived here on earth for me and my family. This is the chapter I knew God would one day make all His own, and sure enough, He did just that. I'm so excited to share it with you too! It seems as though God loves to keep things a mystery, until the perfect moment, then He shows up and displays His glory!

To say the least, I have waited eagerly for this day and to share this part of our story with you. I'm overflowing with joy as I write it because I believe it will cause your spirit to soar with newfound hope and encouragement, as it did mine.

As you know, I never gave up hope or stopped believing God for the victory He promised me from the very beginning of my journey. Although it's been many years since He made that promise, the visual manifestation of my triumphant victory has finally arrived!

Remember earlier, when I quoted what Jesus said to Martha, *Did I not tell you that if you believe, you will see the glory of God?* Well, that's exactly what happened to me! Not only did I live to see His goodness in the land of the living and to hear Him say those glorious words, you have won the victory, but I also saw His glory revealed in my son's lives. However, before I tell this incredible story of victory, I want to share one brief story that I believe will bear witness to a prodigal parent's heart:

I'll never forget the day I watched yet another mom's face light up as she shared with a group about her son's amazing accomplishments. I remember wanting so desperately to tell a similar story about my sons. I went home that day feeling defeated, as I longed to see my day of rejoicing before others over my son's accomplishments too. I knew I needed to encourage myself in the Lord, so I got alone with Him and began praying about my desire to one day boast about my sons' victorious lives as well. Before I knew it, I found myself crying out to Him with a longing heart, "Lord, I want to be proud of my sons like that mother!" With tears running down my face, I pleaded with the Lord. "Please, God, make me proud of them one day!"

After that day, I would often say, right out loud, "Lord, make me proud of them!" As I write this, I'm taken back to that time and the emotions I felt then. Even now it brings tears to my eyes as I recall how desperately I wanted to see my sons' lives restored to God's original plan and purpose.

We read in 2 Corinthians that Paul pleaded with the Lord about a weakness in his life, but God told him, *My grace is sufficient for you, for my power is made perfect in weakness"* (12:9). So Paul said, *Therefore I will boast all the more gladly about my weaknesses, so that Christ's power may rest on me. That is why, for Christ's sake, I delight in weaknesses, in insults, in hardships, in persecutions, in difficulties. For when I am weak, then I am strong* (12:9-10).

Believe me when I say, even to this day I know His grace is sufficient, no matter what circumstances I find myself in. It's during difficult times like these, that we can feel Christ power resting on us, giving us the strength we need to keep on believing. So as I waited desperately for their lives to be restored, I took nothing for granted. Every little baby step my sons made in the right direction was a huge

221

victory for me. For other moms, many of those little things would be taken for granted. But not for me. For example, simple expectations such as their kids getting on through high school or starting college, having a successful business or career, and marring a wonderful Christian woman. I saw each of these achievements as a miracle to believe God for.

I know many of you can relate as parents with prodigals. I knew, from watching the destruction that went on in both of my sons' lives, that seeing these simple blessings would take a miracle from God. I also knew, if they were going to be saved from Satan's evil plot, it would be by the sufficiency of God's grace and power alone.

With that being said, I've already told you about my youngest son's amazing new life with Christ and how God has not only restored him but is using him as an example of hope to restore others. But let me share with you what persistence will do. As I write this, he is now twenty-four, and, keep in mind, he had never attended college before (after barely graduating from high school). Honestly, I don't think he had the confidence to believe he could be a college student, but I knew he could do it. I was his teacher for the first six years of his life. So, as God directed me, I kept pressing him to get enrolled. Finally, after much prayer and encouragement, he finally had the courage to take his first four classes.

Well let me tell you what God-given courage will do. His first grades were two As and two Bs! Glory be to God! The dry bones have risen and a warrior of God is starting to emerge! Not only that, after finishing all of the difficult prerequisites for the registered nursing program, he was recently accepted into the college program. I know he will be one of the most compassionate nurses in his field.

That was my first huge portion of God's faithfulness to His promises--- what a glorious reward! But God wasn't finished yet. Oh no, God promised a double portion in Isaiah 61:7. He said, *Instead of your shame you will receive a double portion, and instead of disgrace you will rejoice in your inheritance.* Now for the story of my double portion—my oldest son (the one who made God laugh).

Remember the mystery I told you about in the beginning, when both I and the prophetess heard God laugh over my son? The mystery God kept hidden and concealed until the appointed time?

It is the glory of God to conceal a thing (Proverbs 25:2 KJV).

Well, that mystery is about to unfold. Yes, this is God's appointed time to display His amazing faithfulness and to reveal the secret that was kept concealed. I must say, when God's appointed time came, His restoring power and how He transfigured our son's life was something incredible to witness.

By the time my son came home from captivity, he was a new man, doing very well in every area of his life with the Lord . . . except in the area that always seemed to trip him up—alcohol. Alcohol was always the place where the enemy would finally entangle him and take him down, and my son knew it would be his greatest struggle when he came home. However, God's word stands true, and something miraculous was about to take place in that area too.

On Easter Sunday, 2015, while the family was gathered at my house for some after-church Easter fun, I noticed my son was sitting alone in my backyard looking completely discouraged. As I walked by him to hide the grandkids' Easter eggs, he looked at me with utter defeat in his eyes. As tears ran down his cheeks he said, "Mom, I'm drinking again."

To this day, I'm not sure of the exact words that came out of my mouth by the Holy Spirit that day, but I do remember not being shaken one bit by what he'd said (which was something supernatural too). As a matter of fact, I never broke eye contact as I spoke the commanded Word of God over him, while simultaneously feeling the power of God surge through me! The words of Isaiah rang out that day: *say to the captives, 'Come out,' and to those in darkness, 'Be free!'* (Isaiah 49:9).

Yes, in that very moment, the Word of the Lord pierced the darkness and set another captive free! Instantaneously, God set him free from all alcohol addiction—he has never craved alcohol since that day.

Immediately, he got up from where he was sitting a completely different man. His countenance glowed with joy as he started playing whiffle ball with the family and having a blissful, victorious day!

So if the Son sets you free, you will be free indeed (John 8:36).

The Son of God rose up on that Easter Sunday and raised another son back to life. Praise God!

Shout to the LORD, all the earth; break out in praise and sing for joy! (Psalm 98:4 NLT).

That same year he married the amazing Proverbs 31 woman I prophesied into his life. He and his wife, now own and operate a very successful business. Also, they recently purchased a beautiful home on a serene, wooded, ten-acre parcel overlooking a two-acre lake. Yes, he accomplished all of these amazing things with the Lord's divine help and guidance. God truly is the rebuilder, restorer, and redeemer of all things!

Let the redeemed of the Lord tell their story—those he redeemed from the hand of the foe (Psalm 107:2).

Then I said: "O LORD, God of heaven, the great and awesome God who keeps his covenant of unfailing love with those who love him and obey his commands (Nehemiah 1:5 NLT).

Our awesome God is faithful to keep His promises. And as wonderful and exciting as my redemption story is for this warrior mother who prophesied by faith to those dry bones, that's not all. Oh, no. Not with our God. Remember when I told you earlier that I knew He would put His own finishing touch on the story? Well, what I'm getting ready to tell you is the Lord's finishing touch. Yes, it is what you call the "much more" of God—a double portion for all our trouble and then some!

Also the Lord gave Job twice as much as he had before (Job 42:10 KJV).

Yes, God's rewards are always above and beyond what we could ever hope for or imagine—like the cherry on top of the perfect sundae. I must say, I never imagined this happening. He not only restored my family, He chose to justify us as well. He wanted to make sure those who'd tried so desperately to destroy us were witnesses as He poured out His manifested glory upon our son's life. You might say, He prepared *a table before us in the presence of our enemies* (Psalm 23:5).

For the eyes of the Lord run to and fro throughout the whole earth, to show Himself strong on behalf of those whose heart is loyal to Him. (2 Chronicles 16:9 NKJV).

It all started one morning in October 2016. On that day, the eyes of the Lord found my oldest son's loyal heart. The local newspaper, which goes out to several local towns in the surrounding area of where we live, ran an article that restored honor to our son. Interestingly enough, it was the same newspaper that ran the first story about him, the one that brought dishonor. And while the first one was meant to disparage my son's name, this one would honor him, without even knowing who he was. The article was titled:

Was he real or was he an angel?

A stranger stops to pray for Calvin Hopper. Two hours later, Hopper is fighting for his life in a hospital.

Written by Wendy Victora.

The family of a man fighting for his life in a local hospital is looking for the stranger who stopped by to pray for him right before he was stricken. Calvin Hopper, whose cancer was in remission, was out in the yard in front of his home Saturday working on his motorcycle.

"You couldn't even tell Daddy was sick," said his daughter Krista Youngberg. "Daddy has hair. Daddy is tan. Daddy looks good."

But out of the blue, a young man stopped by the house.

"Sir, I got the sudden urge to pray for you," the man told Hopper, "Is that OK?"

Hopper was in tears, but told him yes. Two hours later, his family called 911. His blood pressure had dropped so low that his heart was having trouble beating. He was flown to Sacred Heart in Pensacola where he's on life support. Now, the family wants to meet the young man who divined what they hadn't guessed.

"Was he an angel?" Youngberg asked. "Or was he real? If he's real, I just want to talk to him and ask him, 'What did you see? How did you know my Daddy was sick?' His cancer had been in remission for five years!"

His family has asked around to see if anyone might have seen the man who prayed for their father. He is described as being in his 30's, with dark hair and tattoos up and down his arms. He was driving a pick-up truck with a trailer and had been working in Silver Oaks neighborhood.

"Daddy swore that he had met an angel," his daughter said. "He took my daddy's breath away. He thought about this man from the moment he walked in the back door until he was carried away on that stretcher."

A few days later an update was published:

UPDATE: Was he an angel? Or was he real?

The family of a man fighting for his life in a local hospital has found the stranger who stopped to pray with him right before he was stricken.

Written by Wendy Victora

Calvin Hopper, whose cancer was in remission, was out in the yard in front of his Crestview home Saturday working on his motorcycle.

"You couldn't even tell Daddy was sick," said his daughter, Krista Youngberg. "Daddy has hair. Daddy is tan. Daddy looks good."

But out of the blue, a young man stopped by the house. The visitor, who asked that his name not be published, said he'd been praying hard that morning, asking for the Lord to use him in any way that he might be needed.

He'd finished up his work in the neighborhood when he saw Hopper working on his Harley-Davidson. He stopped to talk motorcycles, but the conversation quickly turned to prayer.

"Sir, I got the sudden urge to pray for you," the man told Hopper. "Is that OK?"

Hopper was in tears, but told him yes.

"I could just sense that he needed to be prayed with," the visitor said. "I could definitely sense the Lord's spirit when we were praying together. When I walked away I was shaking."

Two hours later, Hopper's family called 911. His blood pressure had dropped so low that his heart was having trouble beating. He was flown to Sacred Heart Hospital in Pensacola where he's on life support.

Hopper, who just turned 50, is one of six retired Marines who was contaminated by the drinking water at Camp Lejeune in North Carolina in the late '80s, his daughter said. He was diagnosed with cancer five years ago but has been in remission.

Monday morning, the family was able to track down the young man who'd touched their father's life Saturday morning. They had been wondering whether he was an angel, or if he was real.

"Daddy swore that he had met an angel," his daughter said. "He took my daddy's breath away. He thought about this man from the moment he walked in the back door until he was carried away on that stretcher."

The visitor assured Hopper's daughters that he was very real, but that God had brought him to their father's yard. He said he was sad to hear that Hopper had fallen so critically ill.

"I'm a normal person who feels like God used me as a vessel that day," he says. "God was there with us. We both had goosebumps."

***

Unfortunately, Calvin Hopper passed away thirteen days later, but not before being touched by an earthly angel of the Lord. Without a doubt, he saw the glory of God manifested that day through a faithful believer who obeyed God's call to pray. Yes, it's this mama's turn to beam with delight and pride as I tell my son's amazing story—my prodigal son, who God restored and returned home.

The righteous cry out, and the Lord hears them; he delivers them from all their troubles (Psalm 34:17).

Now, let me share with you our son's account of this story, the one the paper didn't have the privilege of printing, the one he later told his Mama and Dad:

I was just having a great day that morning and I asked God to use me in any way He wanted. Right after that prayer, I saw the man out in his front yard, working on his motorcycle; I recognized the bike as one I had seen at the local Harley shop, so I pulled over to ask him if he got it there. He said he had. I told him I could see he had made some cool changes to it and asked if I could come up and take a look at them. He said I could. So I got out of my truck and started talking to him while I looked everything over on the bike. Then I asked him if he was going to the bike rally that was going on in the local area that weekend. He said, "No, I'm going to spend this weekend with my grandkids." So, I just replied, "It looks like you have your priorities straight!"

Immediately, the Lord said, "Ask him if he has his priorities straight with Me." So, I asked the man, "Sir, do you have your priorities straight with God too?" He looked at me with tears in his eyes. Suddenly, I felt the urge to pray with him, so I said, "Sir, I feel a sudden urge to pray for you. Is that OK?" He said yes.

"As I began to pray with the man, the presence of the Lord was so strong, we were both shaking under His powerful presence. To be honest, I can't remember what God spoke through me that day, but when we finished praying, I was still shaking as I walked away. I remember it felt as if my face was glowing like Moses' face was when he came down from the mountain carrying the two tablets of the law in his hands!"

The Word of God says *those who are wise will shine like the brightness of the heavens, and those who lead many to righteousness, like the stars for ever and ever* (Daniel 12:3) As he told us his story, my face radiated too—with joy! Yes, I was bursting with the pride I had once so desperately prayed for. Needless to say, I was blessed beyond measure as I heard how God answered my son's prayer in such a supernatural way that day. A way that brought honor to God's name, and to my son as well.

May the Lord's face radiate with joy because of you (Numbers 6:24-26 TLB).

Remember earlier, when I told you that I believed with all my heart that one day I would see rivers of living water flowing out of my son's heart? Well, now you know what happens when you believe and speak those things that are not, as though they were.

Whoever believes in me, as Scripture has said, rivers of living water will flow from within them" (John 7:38).

As I listened to my son's story, I was reminded of the disciple Stephen, who had a similar experience after Jesus' death. He too was being used by the Lord as a witness, when God's manifested presence appeared and shined upon him, right before he was taken out and stoned to death.

At this point everyone in the high council stared at Stephen, because his face became as bright as an angel's (Acts 6:15 NLT).

I believe this is the glory of God that Jesus promised to those who share in His suffering.

Now if we are children, then we are heirs—heirs of God and co-heirs with Christ, if indeed we share in his sufferings in order that we may also share in his glory (Romans 8:17).

Please understand, I'm not saying that my son has arrived, or that all of my prophesies for him have been fulfilled; nevertheless, I know this to be true…the God *who carries out the words of his servants and fulfills the predictions of his messengers* will bring them to pass at His appointed time! (Isaiah 44:24-26)

Although the test in the demon-possessed valley was long and heart wrenching, the reward—which brought glory to the Lord—was worth it all!

Now all glory to God, who is able, through his mighty power at work within us, to accomplish infinitely more than we might ask or think. (Ephesians 3:20 NLT).

Praise God, now we all know the mystery and what God was laughing about when I asked Him for a son to be used as a minister of God.

The wicked plot against the righteous and gnash their teeth at them; but the Lord laughs at the wicked, for he knows their day is coming (Psalm 37:12,13).

Finally, our time *to proclaim the year of the LORD'S favor and the day of vengeance of our God* against the enemy had arrived (Isaiah 61:2). The Lord saw the Devil's wicked plot against us from the very beginning, and He just laughed at him, knowing his day was coming!.

Endnotes

1. *Merriam-Webster,* s.v. "mandate (*n.*)," accessed 22 May 2019, https://www.merriam-webster.com/dictionary/mandate.

2. *Merriam-Webster*, s.v. "courage (*n.*)," accessed 22 May 2019, https://www.merriam-webster.com/dictionary/courage.

SUGGESTED READING AND VIEWING

Books:

My Utmost for His Highest by Oswald Chambers

The Battlefield of the Mind by Joyce Meyer

Power Thoughts by Joyce Meyer

An Enemy Called Average by John L. Mason

Accessing the Courts of Heaven by Robert Henderson

The Bait of Satan by John Bevere

Art of Hearing God by John Paul Jackson

Videos:

"The Mystery of the Three Dark Nights" by John Paul Jackson

Music:

"Whom Shall I Fear" by Chris Tomlin

"Speak Life" by Toby Mac

"Keep Walking" by Toby Mac

ABOUT THE AUTHOR

Charlotte has faithfully served the Lord since 1980. Referring to herself as "God's highway-byway girl," she has led hundreds of people into the saving knowledge of Jesus Christ, and has trained other Christians to do the same. As an ordained minister, she uses her God given gifts and zeal for the Lord to exhort and build up the Body of Christ. She founded "Jesus Sent Me Ministries" a training center for the "sent ones," a place where they can learn how to share the gospel and fulfill their God-given destinies as victorious warriors of God. Charlotte and her husband Steve, a retired Air Force veteran, currently reside in the Tennessee Smoky Mountains. They have three grown children and three amazing grandchildren.

Please feel free to contact Charlotte and Steve on their ministry website at, JesusSentMeMinistries.org. Also, check out their new and upcoming resources. If you are interested in having Charlotte speak on this topic or teach on evangelism at your church, conference or event, please contact her directly at charlotte@liveinthevictory.com.